CARYLL HOUSELANDER

A BIOGRAPHY

T0283086

Caryll Houselander in the early 1950s. Courtesy Camilla Shivarg.

CARYLL HOUSELANDER

A BIOGRAPHY

Mary Frances Coady

ORBIS BOOKS
Maryknoll, New York 10545

Founded in 1970, Orbis Books endeavors to publish works that enlighten the mind, nourish the spirit, and challenge the conscience. The publishing arm of the Maryknoll Fathers and Brothers, Orbis seeks to explore the global dimensions of the Christian faith and mission, to invite dialogue with diverse cultures and religious traditions, and to serve the cause of reconciliation and peace. The books published reflect the views of their authors and do not represent the official position of the Maryknoll Society. To learn more about Maryknoll and Orbis Books, please visit our website at www.orbisbooks.com.

Manufactured in the United States of America

Library of Congress Cataloging-in-Publication Data

Names: Coady, Mary Frances, author.
Title: Caryll Houselander : a biography / Mary Francis Coady.
Description: Maryknoll, New York : Orbis Books, [2023] | Includes
    bibliographical references and index.
Identifiers: LCCN 2023012178 (print) | LCCN 2023012179 (ebook)
    | ISBN 9781626985308 (print) | ISBN 9781608339884 (ebook)
Subjects: LCSH: Houselander, Caryll. | Catholic authors—England—
    Biography. | Catholic women authors—England—Biography. | Mystics—
    England—Biography. | Women mystics—England—Biography.
Classification: LCC BX4705.H758 C63 2023 (print) | LCC BX4705.H758
    (ebook) | DDC 282.092 [B]—dc23/eng/20230522
LC record available at https://lccn.loc.gov/2023012178
LC ebook record available at https://lccn.loc.gov/2023012179

To the memory of
Margot H. King
1934–2018

Contents

✿

A Rocking-Horse Beginning
(1901–1917)

The nearest one can get to that backward glance from eternity on this earth is, I suppose, to look back across the years to one's childhood.

—Born Catholics

She looked like a medieval saint—or perhaps a medieval tumbler—who had stepped out of a stained-glass window onto the ancient streets of London. So said a friend about the artist and writer Caryll Houselander, who was born in 1901 and died in 1954.[1] Her hair was carrot-colored, cut irregularly in adult years, with a fringe that hung down to her eyebrows. It clashed with the purple smock she donned in her studio. She wore a white substance on her face in adulthood— perhaps a form of cosmetic powder, although another friend said she looked as if she had dipped her face in a bag of flour. As a result, she drew stares. Her round, dark-rimmed glasses sat at a slight angle on her face, giving an off-center look to a small-framed body. Her strange appearance provided the cover for a complex woman who, according to her publisher, had a touch of genius.

Over the course of only fourteen years she wrote books that formed the spiritual reading of choice for monasteries, convents, rectories, and ordinary Catholic households. During those fourteen years Caryll Houselander became the best-selling author for her publisher, Sheed & Ward. Her most popular book, *The Reed of God*, remains a classic. The years immediately preceding the Second Vatican Council were an unlikely period for an unknown English woman of early middle age to become a best-selling Catholic author. Her writing was as clear and sharp and penetrating as that of a medieval mystic, and in fact it has been compared with that of the medieval anchoress Julian of Norwich. It is, perhaps, not a coincidence that the best of it appeared during the Second World War, amid the screech of air-raid sirens and bombed-out devastation, just as Julian's *Revelations of Divine Love* was written during the fourteenth century's Black Death.

Two months before her death, Caryll wrote to her publisher expressing guilt for the tardiness and incompleteness of the autobiography she had been working on. A "real autobiography," she wrote, "would be impossible during the lifetime of my father and my sister"[2]—her mother having died shortly before. Even so, when the short memoir, titled *A Rocking-Horse Catholic*, was finally published in the United States, the husband of Caryll's older sister, Ruth, objected: he had known Caryll for the last thirty years of her life, and he said that she tended to fantasize. She could not be counted on to tell things as they actually were. In the words of a friend, one difficulty with Caryll was the way she reported facts: "with her they hadn't gone through the formality of taking place."[3]

And so—is it fact or fantasy that Caryll came into the world looking like "a tiny red fish"[4] that was not expected to survive, as she claims in *A Rocking-Horse Catholic*? Or that her mother's brother, a gynecologist who had attended the birth, importuned a Protestant clergyman to baptize the infant over a salad bowl? Or that her mother and uncle, when asked the newborn's name, fell into a fit of giggles at the idea that the tiny fish-like thing should be given a name? Or that the baptism was hastily concluded, the infant's names improvised: Frances after her attending uncle and Caryll, after a sailing yacht her mother had been on?

In any event, Frances Caryll Houselander's birth was duly registered as having taken place on September 29, 1901, in the village of Batheaston, near the Roman city of Bath. Caryll's mother, Gertrude Provis, had married Willmott Houselander in Bath in 1898, and Ruth had been born a year later. Gertrude, always known as Gert, came from a well-established merchant and banking family. One relative, Samuel Butler Provis, a barrister, would eventually be knighted by King Edward VII for his work in supervising government-funded charities. Her father, Wilton, became a physician, and her mother, Sarah Easton, had been born in New York City (but about whom little else is known).

Gert, twenty-seven years old at the time of Caryll's birth, was known to be sporty and vivacious, and had grown up in Somerset with a love of outdoor activities, having a special passion for horses. By the time of her wedding, tennis had replaced horses as her main sporting interest. A photograph from 1898 shows her wearing a late Victorian ladies' tennis costume: a generous floor-length skirt and jacket with leg-of-mutton sleeves and bow tie. A narrow-brimmed hat sits no-nonsense style on the top of her head. She holds up the tennis racket: it is a formal pose, and yet the young woman seems ready to give a strong back hand to any ball coming at her. The Victorian age is drawing to a close, a new century is near dawn, the women's suffragette movement is slowly gaining ground, and Gert bears the look of a woman ready to move with the times. She would, in fact, become one of the top female tennis players in England, losing at Wimbledon (in the 1903 quarterfinals) to the champion Dorothea Douglass.

In all likelihood, Gert met Willmott Houselander at a sporting event. He was known to be a huntsman, and had run some of the first point-to-point races in England. It may be that their shared love of the outdoors drew Gert and Willmott together. Six years older than his wife, Willmott grew up in London and followed his father into the banking business, eventually becoming the manager at Wilts & Dorset Bank in Bath. By the time Caryll was born, the family was living in Batheaston, in a substantial house called Fern Cottage. They employed a nursemaid and a cook. The family was vaguely Protestant, but Caryll's assertion in *A Rocking-Horse Catholic*, that her parents "did not believe in or practice any definite religion at all; neither, I think, did they attach the least importance to any"[5] is probably correct.

From the outset, Caryll was called "Baby," and this was the name her family would call her for the rest of her life, her nieces eventually calling her "Auntie Baby." Much later, Ruth's recollection was that, being only two years apart in age, the two sisters "played together quite naturally, she invariably taking the lead because she was the more imaginative."[6] The rocking-horse image of the book's title (as Caryll explained at the outset of the book, she was not a "cradle" Catholic) was taken from a real rocking-horse that she and Ruth shared, a strawberry roan. "His tail came out," Ruth remembered, "and Baby and I were always filling him with things."[7]

The drawing that Caryll made shortly before her death to accompany *A Rocking-Horse Catholic* conjures up a different memory. The drawing is a circle within which a child sits on a rocking horse. The rockers form the bottom of the circle and thus give the drawing the impression of movement. The horse has a wide-eyed demented grin, and a sparse mane consists of a few tufts of hair. The child on its back wears a skirt. Her back is curved forward and her arms, holding onto the reins, are rigid. Her hair flies back from her head. The words of the book's title, A ROCKING-HORSE CATHOLIC, form the circle's rounded top. The impression is of a loop, a circle of terror. The horse is trapped on its runner, the child trapped on the horse, and the whole cycle has no end. (For the book's release after Caryll's death, the unsettling image was greatly tamed when it was replaced by an illustration using the same motif of a rocking horse and child inside a circle.)

In the book's final published version Caryll's description of her early childhood is a contrast to the terror-driven rocking-horse

Caryll's drawing of herself as a "Rocking-Horse Catholic." Courtesy Estae of Margot King.

drawing. In fact, her memory in the book takes her to a lost Eden, replete with kindly people, where her nursemaid, Rose Francis, and her grandfather's groomsman, Bill Reynolds, take center stage. When she first learns of God, Caryll's imagination has God looking exactly like Bill Reynolds. Her picture of heaven is her father's rose garden, which she describes lovingly as "something enchanted and mysterious and unimaginatively beautiful."[8] It is a walled garden, and one enters it through a low wooden door. "When, years later, I heard of the Kingdom of Heaven," she writes, "I imagined one must enter it, if at all, by just such a door, a door just high enough for a child to go through, and a man if he bowed low or went in on his knees, a very low narrow door . . ." and then for a moment she is snapped back into adulthood: she uses the central Christian image that permeates her published work (as if in mid-sentence she reminds herself that there is no heaven without suffering)—"made from the wood of the Cross."[9]

By now it was the Edwardian age, the elderly Queen having died eight months before Caryll's birth and succeeded by her son, Edward VII, but for young children nothing had changed. Caryll's parents, as was the custom where servants were employed, seemed almost nonexistent in her life, and she takes this fact for granted. Not only did she have warm memories of being lovingly cared for, but the memories were sprinkled with an adult's insightful sense of humor (Rose Francis equated Christian virtue with good manners, and "good manners" included not swinging on the garden gate while waiting for the postman, when—as Caryll later learned—Rose wanted the postman's attention to herself.)

Caryll's memory of an idyllic world continues when the family travels to the seaside town of Margate, where Ruth was taken to a sanatorium, having been stricken with tuberculosis. It is not clear how long this trip lasted, but during the sojourn, Caryll and her nurse stayed in the home of her nurse's sister, who had a daughter of about Caryll's age. The child's name was Connie. Caryll's remembered experience of Connie, whom she never saw again after this visit, was similar to her memory of her father's rose garden, only in this case Eden contained a human being. She sets the stage in an image of warmth and love: she and Connie play on the floor in front of a glowing kitchen fireplace, at the feet of Rose Francis and her sister, who sit knitting, their feet in slippers. In this scene, the epiphany is "Connie herself, her fluff of canary hair, her sky-blue dress, her white boots, her odd staggering yet rhythmic gait, and the sound of the spoon rattling in her tin cup . . . and the odd piercing joy of my first conscious awareness of what was, to me at all events, the sheer loveliness of another human being."[10]

In 1905 the family moved to Brighton, on the south coast of England, where Willmott became the manager of the City & Midland Bank. They settled in a house in Hove, a town close to Brighton. Around this time, the nursemaid left the family, and she was replaced by a succession of governesses, some more successful than others. Ruth would remember a game that Caryll liked to play against one of the governesses whom she particularly disliked. The game was called "dead on the stairs," and in it Caryll spread-eagled herself on the steps, pretending to be dead. The governess told her it was wicked to pretend to be dead and that as a punishment there would be no afternoon walk (which Caryll did not want anyway).[11]

Gert's brother was practicing medicine in Brighton at the time, and it was likely through him that the Houselanders met the physician who would become their family doctor. His name was Dr. Frederick Paley. Dr. Paley was the son of Frederick Apthorp Paley, a classics scholar at St. John's College, Cambridge, who under the influence of John Henry (later Cardinal) Newman had converted to Catholicism and as a result had lost his Cambridge position. His son, the medical Dr. Paley, had been educated at the Oratory School founded by Newman in Edgbaston, near Birmingham, and had received his medical degree at St. Bartholomew's Hospital in London. He and his wife, Maud, had three children (twelve-year-old Molly, nine-year-old Frederick Raymond, and six-year-old Graham), whom the Houselander daughters played with. The sacrifice of Dr. Paley's father in giving up an illustrious career in order to become a Catholic had probably left a strong mark on Dr. Paley's own character and led to Caryll's recollection of him as a man of charity and humility who had dedicated his life and his medical practice to the service of the poor.

There was one other person from the Houselanders' Brighton period who would figure prominently in Caryll's life. This was the mysterious figure of George Spencer Bower, a London barrister, who became known to Caryll and Ruth as "Smoky." (His nickname would also be variously spelled "Smokey" and "Smokie.") Smoky, born in 1854, had grown up in a prosperous family in St. Neot's, in Cambridgeshire, and thus by the time he came into Caryll's life he would have been in his early fifties. He had been educated at Winchester College in Hampshire and graduated from New College, Cambridge with first class honors. A scholar of classical literature, he was called to the bar in 1880 and appointed Queen's Counsel in 1903. Smoky had a range of interests in literature and the theater. His first book was a survey called *A Study of the Prologue and Epilogue in English Literature from Shakespeare to Dryden*, and he would go on to write textbooks on several branches of the law. In 1885 he had married Minnie Blanche, the daughter of an actor and theater owner, Charles Culverwell, who had taken the stage name of "Charles Wyndham" and had become one of the best-known theater actors of the day. Smoky enjoyed the company of actors and attended theatrical productions frequently. He and his wife were childless.

It is not known how the Houselanders became friends with Smoky. He and his wife lived in the St. John's Wood district of London, near Regent's Park, and according to Caryll, he spent holiday times living in the Houselander home in Brighton. It seems an odd arrangement, and in her description of the years when Smoky figured in the family's life, she omits any mention of his wife. Nor is it known how exactly he fit into the regular family life of the Houselanders. Caryll's memories of Smoky revert in many ways to the world of idylls—this time, Smoky is the godlike father figure who introduces her to the outside world in the form of classical literature, art, the theater, and, if she is to be believed, Catholicism. Smoky was an agnostic, she tells us, but he was well-versed in church history and Catholic teaching, and regarded the Catholic Church as the repository of all that was beautiful in art and literature. He believed that the Catholic faith was the true one and that if it had not been for the Catholic belief in the Virgin Birth, he would have been baptized. His legal mind was not able to wrap itself around this teaching, and it became such a sticking point for him that he was to remain an agnostic for the rest of his life.

Caryll would correspond with Smoky until the end of his life (she destroyed letters from all her correspondents, and so we have only her side of the few letters to Smoky that have survived). Her first letter to him, perhaps written after Smoky's first visit to Brighton, when he had returned to London, is undated, but is in the hand of a child who is still learning to write:

> My darling Smokey, I do hope you will soon be well because we want you to come down for Christmas because I want to marry you. Our party is on the 27th and Father Christmas is coming himself this time, so you must be here to see him. These are love XX
> Your loving Baby[12]

There is no explanation for the next important thing that happened to Caryll and Ruth—was it Smoky's kindly agnostic influence? Or the Christian example of the Paley family? Gert, the lackluster Protestant, decided that her two daughters should be baptized as Catholics. Ruth was nine years of age and Caryll, three months shy of her seventh birthday. The conditional baptism took place at Sacred Heart Church in Hove on July 16, 1908. Caryll would remember the date for the rest of her life—it was the feast of Our Lady of Mount Carmel—and that, as a small child, she had to stand on a chair so that the baptismal water could be poured over her head. After the baptismal event, life seems to have gone on much as before. Still having two Protestant parents, Caryll would take another few years for her Catholic identity to assert itself. In the meantime, another favorite game that she and Ruth liked to play was "church," which they held in the lavatory, pulling the chain of the toilet as the ringing of the bell.

In 1910 Willmott was transferred to the City & Midland Bank in Bristol, and the family settled in the suburb of Clifton. Soon afterward, on July 12, 1910, Gert was conditionally baptized by Father Robert Stevenson at St. Mary-on-the-Quay Church. At the time, this parish church was served by Jesuit priests. Four months after Gert's reception into the Catholic Church, a Jesuit by the name of George Carolan arrived at St. Mary's. In *A Rocking-Horse*

Catholic, Caryll makes the curious statement: "About this time priests started to frequent our house, where, in spite of his continual unbelief in Catholicism, my father entertained them lavishly."[13]

No doubt these priests included the Jesuit Father Carolan, a native of County Cork in Ireland, who had been ordained a priest for twelve years and had spent his priestly career in teaching and parish work up and down England. At the time of his arrival at St. Mary's parish in Bristol, he was forty-four years old. Father Carolan would figure strongly in Caryll's life over the next few years.

For unknown reasons, whether under the influence of Father Carolan or another priest, or to make an impression on the priests, or perhaps seized by a fit of newfound fervor, Gert, according to Caryll, entered her daughters' lives with a pietistic vengeance. There is no reason to disbelieve Caryll when she writes that her mother insisted that the two girls make little altars and decorate them with Catholic bric-a-brac: statues, candles, and vases of flowers. There was a set of long prayers (she does not mention the rosary, but this could possibly have been one of them) that Caryll and Ruth were made to recite before a particular priest—probably Father Carolan—whom Gert had become particularly fond of. When the adults were out of sight, was when Caryll, so she indicated, said her own private prayers (God "whom I did know to be everywhere, was also localised on my altar"[14]). The piety at home was matched by excessive church-going, at least in Caryll's memory—Mass in their local parish, followed by a High Mass somewhere else on Sundays, and sometimes Benediction after that. Ruth would later claim that her mother had lovers during this time, and possibly Father Carolan was one of them, and the enforced piety was perhaps a means of deflecting neighbors' criticisms. Vague rumors, however, persisted.[15] What the enforced piety did for Caryll was to turn her away from ostentation in prayer.

Around this time an occurrence took place in which Caryll fell ill with an all-consuming physical weakness accompanied by a high temperature and difficulty in breathing. The illness was made worse by hallucinations of guilt and the feeling of a need for her to confess all sins, real and imagined. In *A Rocking-Horse Catholic* she gives the reason for the illness: a visit to a church one day when her father was at work and her mother and sister were away. The church was holding a mission retreat. The retreat master was a member of the Redemptorist Order, which was known at the time for so-called "hellfire and damnation" sermons that gave loud and graphic detail of the horrors of hell if sinners did not repent and seek immediate absolution in Confession. The illness, which Caryll later thought resulted from hysteria, remained undiagnosed, although some later thinking suggests that its origin may have been a physical one.[16]

In late 1912 came the thunderbolt news: Gert and Willmott decided to separate. Decades later Ruth recalled that she, at thirteen, was "much more involved" in the lead-up to their parents' separation than eleven-year-old Caryll, possibly because Caryll, having recently recovered from her serious illness, was still somewhat fragile and kept removed from the discord. Ruth's memory of the disintegrating family atmosphere at the time was: "The parents poured out their complaints of each other to me, vying for my sympathy."[17] In *A Rocking-Horse Catholic* Caryll says that the separation came as a sudden blow, but in the unpublished memoir, "Ghosts and Memories," a long series of poetic verses (which she would later call "rhythms") tell a different story. The first several lines suggest the fragmentation inside the mind and spirit of the sensitive eleven-year-old child who is considered a baby and thus too young to understand. The verses have a desolate ring:

> There was a whispering in the house—
> "for the sake of the children!"
> There was a whispering on the stairs,
> whispering in the chink of the door,
> whispering in the curtains,
> whispering in the cupboards;
> the house was whispering,

whispering like the flitter of mice . . .
"For the sake of the children,
for the children's sake!"
whispering, whispering, whispering,
like the flitter of mice the whisper of lies. . . .[18]

The verses go on for several dozen lines. The two sisters never spoke to each other of their parents' breakup or the new turn their lives were taking. Home as they had known it no longer existed. Their destination was now a convent boarding school. On January 13, 1913, they were put on a train to Birmingham, and from there to the nearby town of Olton. There they were admitted to the Convent of Our Lady of Compassion, known familiarly as the Olton Convent. It was run by nuns who had come from France in recent years, possibly to escape the anti-clerical laws in that country.

It is not known when Caryll's eyes had begun to need correction, but by the time she arrived at the Olton Convent, she was wearing eyeglasses. Fellow boarders at the convent would remember Caryll's distress during that period, her slight stature, her pallor, and her thin straight copper-colored hair, her main comfort being the teddy bear that she called "Roosy," which she had received at the age of six when the family was on holiday in the seaside town of Bournemouth, in Dorset. (The stuffed bear would remain with her until her death.)

After her initial unhappiness, Caryll grew to love the Olton Convent. In describing it, she reverts to the idyllic language she used in recalling her early childhood. Everything was sparkling and full of sunshine in the convent—the look of dazzling sheets in the white dormitory, the kindness of the nuns, the smell of lemon and soap when she came close to one particular nun. In fact, the convent, like all Catholic boarding schools of the period, was run like a little monastery. Regularity governed each day: daily Mass, regular hours for schoolwork and for meals. Children sat at the same place for each meal and were required to keep their beds and desks tidy at all times. There were periods of silence, and edifying readings took place at mealtimes. "Good manners" were taught, and every minute of the day was to be spent in some useful pursuit. Sewing and knitting were taught to the girls. After the chaos of home life, this regular discipline was what Caryll needed in order to thrive. The feast days of the Church were joyous occasions, with treats at mealtime and special privileges allowed. The convent became the Houselander girls' home, even during the holiday periods. As at a regular home, there were chores such as collecting eggs from the hens and pounding plums to make jam.

During her first months at the Olton Convent, and probably before, Caryll wrote poetic verses and accompanied them with thumbnail sketches. It was no doubt an important gratification to her, given her budding creative life, that she not only felt free to submit her written work and her drawings to the school paper, *The Oltonian*, but that these were accepted and printed. One offering from eleven-year-old Caryll shows an unusual sensibility and an already keen sense of humor, as well as a droll acknowledgment that she had no musical inclination:

The Music Pupil

THE PIANO
I have tried at C, I've tried at A,
But the right note I cannot play.
I can't play a flat, I can't play a sharp,
I'll give it up, and play the harp.
THE HARP
On the notes my fingers shake,
The strings they always seem to break;
The way I hold it is all wrong,
I cannot play a single song.
For me to play is quite a sin,
I think I'll try the violin.

THE VIOLIN
Alas, alas, I've tried in vain,
And I will not try again;
I might as well cry for the moon
As try to play a single tune.
MORAL—Before the great attempt the small,
And so in time accomplish all.

Another poem, a nine-stanza ode to Roosy, appeared in the same issue of the school paper:

Roosy (My Teddy Bear)

1.
His height is just one foot,
His eyes are black as soot,
He used to have much hair
But now he's nearly bare
His temper is quite strange
It always seems to change,
But he's been a faithful friend
To me from start to end. . . .[19]

During the early summer of 1914, the French nuns at the Olton Convent paid particular attention to the alarming reports of military escalation coming across the English Channel. Then, on August 3, came the news everyone was dreading: Britain declared war against Germany. At the Olton Convent, this was not an abstract reality happening to people far away. Many of the nuns spoke about their bitter experiences during the Franco-German war several decades earlier, and when news came in late September of the wanton destruction of parts of Rheims Cathedral in northern France by German shellfire, anti-German fervor was raised to fever pitch. At the same time, tales reached across the Channel of atrocities committed in Belgium. Belgian refugee children began to arrive at the convent. Caryll's patriotic writing was encouraged, and it was a source of pride and accomplishment to her when a nun composed music for one of her verses.

Shortly after the appearance of reports that compared Germans to savage "Huns," Caryll, now aged thirteen, had the first of three unusual experiences which she wrote about in *A Rocking-Horse Catholic*. She had no satisfactory descriptive word for these strange happenings except that she saw them with her *mind*, not with her eyes. In Caryll's brief account of the first experience, it had to do with the convent's lone German nun, who, in Caryll's written telling, remained nameless (her name was Sister Mary Benedicta). At the time of the Olton Convent, some orders of nuns were divided into two classes: "choir sisters" did the work requiring training and education, such as teaching; "lay sisters," often having little education, did housework and kitchen and laundry duties. In girls' boarding schools the lay sisters acted as servants. They often cleaned up after the children, took care of their clothing and even washed the children's dishes after meals. The nun in Caryll's account was a lay sister. She spoke English badly, and unlike the cultured French nuns who taught at the school, she did not, according to Caryll, excel in anything.[20]

On the day of Caryll's particular encounter with her, the nun was polishing the boarders' shoes in the boot room. As Caryll came closer to her, she saw tears running down the nun's cheeks. Too embarrassed to make eye contact, the girl looked down at the nun's rough, chapped hands and the child's shoe she was polishing. When she looked up, Caryll saw on the nun's head a crown of thorns. The vision—if that was what it was—lasted only a few seconds. In her essay written for Frank Sheed's anthology, *Born Catholics*, Caryll described the experience more fully: It was "more like a cap of thorns, covering her head, and so heavy that it bowed it down."[21] "I shall not attempt to explain this," Caryll wrote in *A Rocking-Horse Catholic*. "I am simply telling the thing as I saw it."[22]

During the next months, when food shortage became a problem, meals at the Olton School were unappetizing and in general not especially nourishing. Caryll began a secret regimen of starving herself, whether because physically she could not stomach the food, or as a means of rebellion and anger. (Roosy the teddy bear was her constant companion, and she pretended to be feeding him under the table instead of herself.) News of the war just across the English Channel filtered continually into the convent, and a school friend remembered that Caryll's creative writing dealt a lot with war images.

In the early months of 1915 she also began experiencing abdominal pains. It is not clear whether her mother was summoned to the convent (Gert and Willmott both disappear from this part of Caryll's own narrative) or whether help was sought by some other means, but in March 1915 Caryll was taken to London, where her mother was now scraping out a living, and where appendicitis was diagnosed. Her mother's brother conducted the surgery. After her recovery, she was sent to a series of Protestant schools near her mother, but at each one she felt dislocated, a stranger, unable to fit in. She seems not to have fully recovered from the surgery, and perhaps the hormonal changes of puberty exacerbated her condition. Both *A Rocking-Horse Catholic* and her short memoir in *Born Catholics* indicate her sense of being not only "singular," but "a freak" during these teenage years. Decades later, Ruth would write: "My sister was 'a natural oddity' and could never have fit into any community."[23] Yet for a girl of fourteen, not to be able to fit in and make friends would have been a disconcerting, and perhaps deeply lonely, experience.

It may have been desperation that drove Gert to consult Dr. Paley, the Houselanders' former family doctor in Brighton who had had such a formative influence on the family and on Caryll in particular. The decision was made that Caryll would be admitted to a convalescent home in Brighton under the care of Dr. Paley. The Paley family renewed acquaintance with the thin, pale, disconnected teenager. Molly Paley, in particular, now in her early twenties, took Caryll under her wing, and they would remain friends well into adulthood.

In January 1917, Caryll was admitted to the Convent of the Holy Child in St. Leonards-on-Sea, on the coast of Sussex, near Hastings. The sea air was thought to be suitable for a girl who was still convalescing. This convent, which had been established by the Society of the Holy Child Jesus, was bigger than the Olton Convent, and although she grew to respect both the nuns and the other girls, fitting in was not easy. Girls were expected to be outgoing and to enjoy sports, to be apple-cheeked and robust. To be like Gert. "Singularity" was frowned upon, and in the atmosphere of "let's all be a jolly lot," Caryll writes that she became "too acutely self-conscious, too aware of myself as a freak."[24] She also perceived an ethos of snobbery, a type of English Catholicism that prided itself on being part of polite and acceptable society. In later life she reflected on this reality as a failing in Christian charity, but at the time she was likely aware that her family—her parents separated, her mother earning a living at odd jobs, her father absent from her life—would not have fit into the category of what were considered "good" (that is, well-to-do and respectable) families. She took refuge in letters to Smoky. In one she griped that it was "too sickening" that "the girls never seem to read Hamlet except as a Penance—to think of a poet giving the treasures of his mind to be a delight, a pleasure, a consolation—and they turn this to punishments for naughty little school girls."[25]

In another letter to Smoky she laid out all the faults, as she saw them, of her fellow students. According to her recollection in *A Rocking-Horse Catholic*, she added a complaint about the "prefect," or nun in charge of the boarders: "Mother So-and-so thinks that she is the cock of the walk here."[26] According to her account, she submitted her letter in an unsealed envelope (according to the custom of the time), to be read by the nun in charge. The nun handed the letter back to her and said, "I won't let this go because I can't let you say such unkind things about the children that I love."

Caryll Houselander at the age of sixteen. Courtesy the Utley family.

The nun added, according to Caryll, who was red-faced with shame, "About myself, you are right. I am the cock of the walk here, so there is nothing to be done about that but to make the best of it." She told Caryll to rewrite the letter, stating the same grievances if she wanted, "but more justly and more kindly."[27] Then, when Caryll handed her the rewritten letter, the nun sealed the envelope without reading the contents. (The nun's name was Mother Aloysia. Many years later, upon her death in 1971, she would be described as a nun who "believed in discipline and in imposing it with some severity, but she inspired respect by her utter sincerity and her prayerful spirit; the children might be rather scared of her but they knew they could trust her and that she loved and respected them as children of God, especially some of the more difficult ones whom she was often able to understand

and help.")[28] It says something about Caryll, knowing that Mother Aloysia would read the letter, that not only was she not frightened of this nun, but she actively provoked her. It is likely that Caryll was one of the "difficult" students whose "singularity" Mother Aloysia understood, and the nun would continue to figure greatly in Caryll's life for the next several years. They would remain friends until Caryll's death. A few years after Caryll left St. Leonards, the school would inaugurate an annual magazine called *The St. Leonards Chronicle*, and during the course of the 1920s Caryll would contribute six poems to the publication. She would also visit the nuns, sometimes staying a few days.

Caryll remained friendless at St. Leonards because, according to Mother Aloysia in later years, the other girls in the boarding school did not understand her.[29] But for Ruth, the Holy Child Convent, which she attended at Cavendish Square in London, was a godsend. She did very well in her studies and with the help of one of the Sisters was admitted to Oxford University to study history. She would eventually become a magistrate and the chair of the Tower Bridge Juvenile Court.

School days, however, were soon to come to an end for Caryll. According to the convent's records, Caryll left the school at Christmas of 1917. She was now sixteen. According to Caryll herself, Gert had decided it was time for her to enter the world of work.

2

Summoned to London
(1918–1922)

At this time I had given up going to Mass and was looking for some form of Christianity other than Catholicism.
—Born Catholics

By early 1918 Caryll was living with her mother in a flat at 138 Portsdown Road in the district of Maida Vale, in west London. The purpose in her recall from the convent school, according to *A Rocking-Horse Catholic*, was to help Gert with the housework. A third person, however, was living in the flat as well. This was Father George Carolan, the Jesuit who had become a friend of Gert's in Bristol.

During the period prior to Caryll's return to live with her mother, Father Carolan had experienced several bouts of ill health. In March 1917, he had suffered an attack of severe abdominal influenza and spent several weeks recuperating. His mental health may have begun to deteriorate as well. At some point he requested permission to leave the Jesuits, and formal dismissal was granted in August 1917. Although he remained a priest of the diocese of Bristol, Father Carolan suffered from a number of unspecified medical problems over the next several years, and it is unlikely that he served as a diocesan priest after leaving the Jesuits.

If Caryll's account in *A Rocking-Horse Catholic* is to be believed, there was considerable friction in the household, especially between herself and Father Carolan. If a man with a mental disorder who was used to having his own way ruled the household in the small space of a flat, as she indicates, one can understand that conflict would ensue. It makes sense as well that neighbors' eyebrows would have been raised when it became known that a woman who was separated from her husband had a Catholic priest living with her.

Caryll would tell friends in later years that her mother had taken in the priest out of pity and that there was nothing more to their relationship than that. For the remainder of his life, Father Carolan would be in and out of convalescent homes, but his address would continue to be Gert's house, even when she moved to 12 Boundary Road, which she ran as a boardinghouse. He would die of anemia on December 13, 1926.

Meanwhile, across the English Channel, there was no indication that the war would end in a few months. The fighting remained fierce and brutal as the Germans gained strength in their advance toward Paris. Zeppelin attacks still occurred, and in March 1918 a German bomb fell on a residential building in Maida Vale, killing twelve people and damaging four hundred houses.[1] No record remains as to whether this attack had an effect on Gert Houselander's household arrangement.

By the end of that month, Caryll was in Bath at a guesthouse run by relatives of Gert's, writing to Smoky. The letter reflects the sentiments of an angry teenager, bent on rebellion and criticizing everything in her wake, whether justifiably or not, making assumptions about the people around her, supposing herself superior to them. (It also reflects the vulgarity of style that Caryll would employ throughout her life in casual conversation.) In a sense, as well, it is a *cri de coeur* thrown out to the only person who understands her:

I've made a thousand attempts here to write a poem, a poem about the wind in the trees that crown the big hill behind this godforsaken house. But it's no use. If I sit in the drawing room I'm cleared out—if I sit in the dining room they turn me away to lay the table—so I wander all round the house fit to blub with irritation. These damned old righteous self-satisfied, cold-footed old hags who inhabit Bath ought to be put into the ethereal chamber without exception and the pale soury-faced curates along with them, and then put some young people to live here. Some people who love the storm that bends and twists the weird grand trees on the hill tops and hear their own voices shouting with exaltation—Let's have young limbs who will run up these hills and laugh at the wild black clouds that flood the skies. Let's knock down these musty, fusty houses and go out to live with the splendour out there. And these chicken-livered asses here spend their lives indoors, reading cookery books, knitting lace, grousing at the grand free splashing rain, giving themselves and everybody else most acute tummy-ache.

There isn't even a decent book here except one, that's "The Idylls of the King" and I'm sure that it got in by mistake. It looks so out of place that I giggle whenever I see it. I try to keep amicable—it's very hard though and necessitates a lot of working off steam in various ways—i.e. Swedish drill in my bedroom and Limericks with bad language in them silently and secretly composed during meals. Of course one pities these sort of old fools. They have never had a day's really good fun in their lives. They have taken all their stuffy meals round stiff tables, never sat on the floor in their lives, never been out without gloves—never ever touched lovely soft grass in their lives.[2]

By the summer of 1918, the fighting on the continent was as ferocious and all-consuming as it had ever been. Caryll's second unusual psychic experience took place one day in July, four years after the first. According to her account, she was on her way to a store to buy potatoes when she was stopped on the sidewalk by what she later described as "a gigantic and living Russian icon" that rose above her. It was an elaborate image of Christ the King stretched out on a fiery cross, bejeweled and crowned with gold. The image filled the sky, Christ's arms "reaching, as it seemed, from one end of the world to the other." The eyes of the image "stood sharp with grief,"[3] but the mouth smiled, as if absorbing the sorrow inside it.

The image lasted only a short while, and then Caryll resumed her shopping. Not long afterward, she read in the newspaper that the czar of Russia and all his family had recently been assassinated. The image she had seen eventually became for her a symbol of the shedding of the blood of a king, the people's anointed leader. The contrast, and also the similarity, between the crown of gold and the crown of thorns on the humble nun from years earlier would eventually become clear to her. Shortly before her death, she wrote, "I knew suddenly that Christ is in kings as well as in outcasts, that His Passion in the world today is being lived out in kings as well as in common men."[4]

Smoky had been her one consolation since her move back to her mother's house in London. She visited him every week and wrote to him when she was away. A scant month after her vision of the crucified tsar, she was visiting the Paley family in Sussex and wrote:

It is a long while since we have missed a Sunday together and tea in your garden and the little wash up that Nursey and I indulge in after it. The one "wash up" in life which causes me pleasure, and which generally splashes me all over as I always turn on the taps at full tilt and forget them through talking so hard until I am all splashed—and Nurse's voice says, "Oh Baby, look at your dress." It's been a little storm here but that delights me personally. The storm is a splendid great fellow; he has eyes that glint like rusty flames and long dark hair that spreads over the sun and huge limbs, and he shakes torrents out of the trees. I always long to be just a part of the storm when the rain is just over and the storm is gently moving over the thick trees, shaking a few drops out of them very gently; then wee squirrels come out and look around with keen little killing eyes and hop over the lawn and on to the wall. And the birds fill the silence, blackbirds with their few wonderful notes which are nicer (to me) than any bird I've heard, and I know you love them too . . .

Of course it is lovely to be with Molly [Paley] again. Smoky, she is so sweet, you can say any rot to her and she understands, and you can say nothing at all to her and she understands, which is even better, then she says goodnight to me when I'm in bed and you know being said goodnight to in bed is my greatest joy in life. I sleep simply glowing with content when Molly has performed that ceremony. . . . Just now Molly is curled up on a sofa trying to sleep, she says she suffers intensely from what she called "the glare" which is only my occasional affectionate glances at her.[5]

On November 11 the armistice was signed, the guns fell silent across the English Channel, and the Zeppelin raids stopped. Caryll had just turned seventeen. Over the next few years significant changes were to come into her life, but it is impossible to pinpoint the exact sequence of events. In *A Rocking-Horse Catholic* she writes of an elderly, unnamed artist who befriended her and arranged for her to attend the St. John's Wood Art School in North London, even though she claimed at the time that she was more interested in writing poetry than in creating visual art. (The art school, distinguished in its time, eventually became the Anglo-French Art Centre, and no official records of it have been left.)

In London, bohemianism—the prewar alternate lifestyle in dress and living arrangements and freedom of expression—took on a new articulation with the postwar generation: clubs emerged in Soho, and there were cocktails and cigarettes, and women cut their long hair short, raised their skirts, and the more daring began wearing trousers. It was a new world for Caryll, and despite her shyness and what she had regarded as her "singularity," she entered it fully. She made friends at the art school, and in later years some of them remembered her love of the new jazz-age dances. Together with a small group of friends, she formed "The Cheerful Idiots," a society of art students that included "impromptu dancing and general revelry," she wrote to Smoky, "and we gather round a vast and smoky stove and tell each other stories, also true incidents much exaggerated, and laugh ourselves nearly into fits."[6] The smoky stove was inside a wooden hut that Caryll and her friends arranged to have built in the garden of the Boundary Road house where she still lived with her mother. The hut became an art studio that they christened "Spooky."

This was the throwing-off of the convent-school world. It also represented the rejection of the Catholic Church that Caryll had been baptized into. In *A Rocking-Horse Catholic* she gives the details of her decision to walk away from Catholicism at this time of her life: the insistence at one church that she pay for a place to kneel and sit, and what she sensed was a general hypocrisy among the Catholic faithful themselves, as when two acquaintances of herself and her mother refused to speak to her immediately after Mass at which all had just received communion. She would also remember the lack of charity that she felt had been visited upon Father Carolan by Catholics, including his fellow priests.

A letter to Smoky written in June 1919, from the Kent seaside town of Herne Bay, shows Caryll trying to work out a new belief system:

I have read Shelley's "Ode to the West Wind" and loved it beyond words. But not Kingsley's "Ode to the North Easter." I must get hold of it and so though I love all the winds, and am in absolute sympathy with the old man in the novel you tell me about who upholds the theory of the oneness of human beings and the elements—that is exactly my own creed, that God is the Spirit and Soul of Nature and that we are all part of the matter of nature, but the more spiritual we become, the more we get unified with the Spirit of Nature and gradually become absorbed in God. I think the earth a living thing. I go and talk to it, and I think it would be presumptuous to set up myself, who am made of dust, as at all higher or even as high as the beautiful living earth that has God for a soul. I don't hate the thought of "dust to dust" but rather like to think of being part of a thing so broad and splendid and fertile as the earth.

I shall devote all my art, poetry, and painting to this one cause, to lead people to live in union with Nature; I think they can all their lives and when they are dead, they will have to . . .

Did I tell you that Mummy has taken to golf again with great fury? I went up and had a shot at it one day and broke a golf club over it and used some murky oaths, and caused Mummy to use a few too by exclaiming on the beauty of the surrounding country just as she was about to drive. Then I lost a few balls and hacked up a goodly portion of the green and finally sat on the top of a bunker and surrendered. I am afraid I lack the sporting characteristics of the English man, for it has always been a matter of profoundest wonder to me how a free thinking, independent, intellectual, bumptious Saxon can voluntarily become a complete slave to a damned little white ball and go blindly after it round eight or nine miles of artificially bumpy country on a sweltering summer's day, swearing and cursing and fighting with his best pal over it all the way round! It just baffles me.[7]

By now, Ruth was studying at Oxford, and from time to time she brought home fellow students. One was a young man named Henry Andrews. At the time Caryll met Henry he was in his mid-twenties, "rather like a tall giraffe, sweet, kind and loving,"[8] according to the novelist Rebecca West, who later married him. Henry had an exotic background, having been born in Rangoon, Burma, of a British father and a mother of mixed European heritage. He had begun studies in Oxford, but had found himself in Germany when the war broke out. He was imprisoned in an internment camp, and so he had returned to finish his university degree only in 1919.

Caryll, right, with her sister, Ruth Morrah and Ruth's daughters, Dierdre and Brigid, 1928. Courtesy the Utley family.

Caryll became briefly engaged to Henry. One can see why she should become attracted to a man of such an unusual blend of experience and family background as well as gentleness of spirit, and she enjoyed dancing with him (he paid for her to take ballroom dancing lessons at Marguerite Vacani's dance school, later to become famous for giving dance lessons to royalty). But besotted as she was with her new freedom-loving lifestyle and the feeling of living on the edge of society (which would never quite leave her), it was obvious that such a match would not take hold.

Another friend was Molly Ackland, later known as the poet Valentine Ackland. Molly's sister, Joan, was a friend of Caryll's at the art school, and Molly recalled meeting Caryll as a young and unhappy adolescent. Caryll was introduced to her at first as "Houselander," because the art students called each other only by last name. She remembered Caryll as "tiny, thin, shy, impulsive. She used to write me long, long letters, to which I replied. . . . She taught me to read Blake and Shelley and Whitman—she also talked to me a great deal about 'Anarchists' and told me she was one. I was impressed and at once decided to be an Anarchist myself, without much idea of what they were. She used to come down from St. John's Wood to St. James's Court in Westminster, where I lived with my disapproving parents, and sometimes had breakfast with me, and often she and I walked together in St. James's Park, or prowled about on the flat roof of our block of flats. I had an armless and legless wooden doll, a Russian doll, at that time: Caryll (she told me to call her that) used to write letters to it, I remember."[9]

A friend whose connections had a more lasting impact on Caryll was a young woman by the name of Eleanor Toye. Eleanor was eight years older than Caryll. She had grown up in an upper middle-class household (her father was a master at Winchester College) and spent the war years working in the War Office in London and then in the passport office in Madrid. She was also a sometime singer, and Caryll seems to have met her through her art school friends. Little is known about Eleanor's activities during this time, but it could be that she had become an agent for the British

Secret Intelligence Service, or SIS (forerunner of MI5 and MI6).

At some point during their friendship, Eleanor became the secretary to a man named Sidney Reilly. Through her, Caryll met Reilly, and a relationship developed between them, but no more is known about it than that simple fact. Reilly was a British spy with a murky background. Born in Russia around 1874 with the name Shlomo (or Sigmund) Georgievich Rosenblum, he was at least twenty-five years older than Caryll, and so at the time they met she was barely out of her teens (if that) and he was in his mid-forties. Reilly had spent his early adult years as an adventurer, and from there he moved into intelligence work, for which he had a particular aptitude, in part because of his talent for languages and also because of a certain penchant for danger. His chameleon-like past also worked in his favor (although the SIS would eventually come to regard him as untrustworthy). He had been sent to Russia in 1917 with a plan to overthrow the new Bolshevik government. The plot was discovered, but Reilly managed to escape back to England on a false passport and was awarded the Military Cross in 1919. In Russia, however, he was found guilty *in absentia* of espionage and sabotage and was sentenced to be shot.

This daring, mysterious spy was also said to have been a womanizer—and, in much later years, one of the models for the James Bond novels by Ian Fleming. A charming and witty conversationalist, Reilly was an impeccable dresser and comported himself elegantly. He reportedly already had at least one mistress by the time he married a wealthy Irish widow by the name of Margaret Thomas in 1898. Margaret's first husband, a clergyman, had died under strange circumstances. Stories about his death vary, all involving Reilly in some way: in one, Reilly attended the sick man, pretending to be a doctor; in another, Reilly, posing as a pharmacist, had come to their home with the husband's prescriptions. All stories seem to agree that the man's body was hastily buried after Dr. T. W. Andrew examined the corpse and declared him dead. Only later was it discovered that no medical doctor by that name existed. A decade later, Margaret disappeared from Reilly's life, later claiming that he wanted to get rid of her. They never divorced. Next, he entered into a bigamous marriage with a Ukrainian woman named Nadine Massimo. He did eventually get a divorce from this wife. When Caryll entered his life, he likely had a succession of mistresses and perhaps had gone through a second bigamous marriage.

It is difficult to picture Caryll as having anything to do with a man who had such an out-sized, spy-novel background. To what extent did Caryll, carrot-haired, bespectacled, plainly dressed and impecunious, consort with this man? Reilly was said to be attracted to women with red hair, however, and it may have been this feature that he liked in her. Or perhaps the ability she had cultivated to take part in amusing conversation, along with a gift for mimicry, as well as a reputation among her friends for clairvoyance through the use of handwriting analysis that she had begun to learn as an art student. Dermot Morrah, a fellow Oxford student of Ruth's (whom she would marry in 1923), claimed many years later that Caryll was living as Reilly's mistress and that the spy "made her a weekly allowance, small but quite adequate to her simple manner of life."[10] Other friends saw Reilly as merely fascinated with Caryll because at the time she was testing out various religions and had a particular preoccupation with Russian Orthodoxy, as he did. These friends claimed that the money he gave her were for her drawings.

It seems clear that Caryll fell in love with Reilly—or at least formed a passionate erotic attachment to him. According to Reilly's first biographer, Robin Bruce Lockhart, whose father had been sent to Russia with Reilly in 1917, "Reilly meant a great deal more to Caryll than she did to him, but his love for her was perhaps the most spiritual of his life."[11] Caryll was, according to Lockhart, "an essential part of his life in London."[12] Another biographer claimed: "With the purity of her face and her long red hair cut in a bang across her forehead, she made him think of another Joan of Arc."[13]

Caryll spoke of being torn apart when, in 1923, Reilly married (again, bigamously) an actress with the stage name of Pepita Bobadilla and again when she heard that he had been killed in Russia in 1925. Sometime after that, while on a visit to Germany,

Caryll wrote, "[T]here is a man here who has a note in his voice like Sidney; he is Hungarian. I am obliged to talk to him often and it twists my heart to do so. After all these years of driving back the thought of Sidney, I am still so weak that I cannot see the faintest likeness to him in anyone without feeling as if my whole life is an open wound."[14] A few years later she would write a poem in his memory:

> To S.G.R. Killed in Russia
> Pure Beauty, ever-risen Lord!
> In wind and sea I have adored
> Thy living splendour and confessed
> Thy resurrection manifest.
> Not now in sun and hill and wood,
> But lifted on this bitter rood
> Of man's sad heart, I worship Thee
> Uplifted once again for me.
> For now the Jews cast lots again
> On thy raiment, mock Thy pain,
> And make Thy torments manifold,
> Selling Thee again for gold.
> I bow to Thee in this new shrine,
> This later calvary of Thine,
> And in the soul of this man slain
> I see Thee, deathless, rise again.[15]

Years later, in a letter to a friend who had just split up with a man, she wrote, "I know what it feels like to part from a man whom one is in love with, for I too have done so, years and years ago—and the years have not lessened or dimmed the love, even though he is dead now, shot in Russia by the Communists. I know what anguish such a parting can be."[16] Sidney Reilly's photograph sat on Caryll's bedside table until her death.

Adding to the mystery of Reilly and his legendary way with women, Eleanor Toye, his secretary, wrote to Robin Bruce Lockhart when Lockhart was researching the biography: "I do not think that Reilly was ever wholly involved with women. His political activities were what really mattered to him. I knew him well but there was no sentiment or sex in the relationship. He was an extraordinarily good friend and generous to a fault to those whom he liked. From my experience, he was essentially a man of great integrity. . . . Apart from the personal details I have mentioned about Reilly, I would add that he was a dynamic personality and had apparently inexhaustible energy. An example of his good heartedness was when he allowed a young friend of mine whom he considered very talented, three pounds a week for twelve months for study, after asking her mother's permission. This girl, who is now dead, idolized him and kept a photograph of him constantly with her. She eventually became a well-known writer on religious subjects. Sex certainly played no part in their friendship. I don't know how reliable he was politically, but personally I had a great deal of respect for him as a man. He did me many kindnesses and gave me good advice. I shall always remember him as one of the most vivid personalities I have ever known." In a PS, Eleanor Toye wrote: "She made a sort of god of Sidney and thought that he had descended straight from Heaven!"[17] She later added that the "young friend" was Caryll Houselander.[18]

At some point during these years of the early 1920s, Caryll moved out of her mother's home and rented a room in another boardinghouse. She took on a series of low-paying jobs. She worked as a commercial artist for a time, as well as a charwoman, which, due to an extreme fear of mice, she could not hold onto for long. She babysat, wrote love letters for men who were unable to express their feelings, and did sound effects for an acting troupe (in a rare display of the humor that friends would later remember about her, she writes that her off-stage specialties were "sound of a cock crowing" and "sound of a husband and wife quarrelling"[19]). She continued to roam the streets looking for churches that might satisfy her spiritual longings.

She speaks in *A Rocking Horse Catholic* of her love for Jewish liturgy and the turmoil she felt over not fitting in to any religion, as well as her desire to return to Catholicism if only she could find Christianity in it. Around this time, her third strange psychic encounter took place. Like the other two, it happened in the most mundane of circumstances. She was riding on an underground train at the end of a work day. The train was crowded, people jostling one another as it sped along, rattling noisily. Suddenly Caryll saw the people around her as Christ, and not only those on either side of her, not just all the people on the train itself, but all people everywhere, living and dead. This sense of the shared participation of all humanity in the life of Christ—in his suffering and in his glory—lasted, she writes, for several days. After that, it was a matter of blind faith: "Christ was hidden again."[20]

But from then on it was just a matter of time before she would find her way back into communion with the Catholic Church again.

3

Search for God
(1923–1929)

Christ is everywhere; in Him every kind of life has a
meaning and has an influence on every other kind of life.
—A Rocking Horse Catholic

The path of Caryll's return to Catholicism was likely long and unsure at first. The Catholic Church in England that she came to as a young adult woman was, in a sense, fraught, having had a tortuous history ever since the Reformation four centuries earlier. The Catholic Emancipation Act, which allowed British Catholics to take full part in public life, was not yet quite a hundred years old, having been proclaimed only in 1829. The diocesan episcopacy, nonexistent in Britain since the reign of Queen Elizabeth I, was reestablished only twenty years after that. The history of persecution of Catholics was highlighted by the stories of Thomas More and John Fisher (both beatified only in the late nineteenth century) as well as the memory of those who had been executed for their faith during Elizabeth I's reign. The sense of being second-class citizens in their own country contributed to a siege mentality on the part of Catholics. This mentality underscored an ultramontane view of the Catholic Church, in which Catholics generally looked unthinkingly to Rome and the Pope for approval and direction in all matters religious and spiritual.

There had been a move, especially in France, in the late nineteenth century, for the Church to look beyond itself and to engage with the modern age in the light of the scientific findings of recent decades. The movement, given the term "Modernism," was condemned by the Church. As a result, a British Jesuit named George Tyrell, who had pleaded with Church authorities to adopt an open approach in its engagement with modern society, was expelled from the Jesuits and excommunicated from the Church. This treatment toward Tyrell, which some Jesuits considered overly harsh, cast a chill over attempts at new theological ideas within Catholicism. Pious devotions, which did not threaten the status quo, were encouraged among the faithful. A spiritual martyrdom of sorts also existed as a result of the Oxford Movement: some well-placed people—John Henry Newman the most prominent and Dr. Paley's father among them—had converted to Catholicism and had suffered for it by losing their university positions as a result of their conversion. These people gave Catholicism a patina of courage to the point of sacrifice.

Although ultramontanism dictated the religious lives of Catholics, a new spirit was bubbling up among educated Catholics in Britain, eventually to be known as "the Catholic intellectual revival."[1] The Catholic Evidence Guild was founded in 1918 to present a clear, public explanation of Catholic doctrine. The new publishing company of Sheed & Ward would soon be the outward face of this revival, but for the time being it would pass Caryll Houselander by.

In 1922, her old convent school, St. Leonards, inaugurated an annual magazine called *The St. Leonards Chronicle*, and in 1924 it published a poem of Caryll's called "Easter":

Easter

The slim green tapers on the hills,
Are lit, the glimmering daffodils

Profuse with sweet and sudden light,
The purple-hooded eremite
Has quit His mantle of the night;
Revested, goes in white and blue
Bearing chalices of dew.
Relit the altar flame that glows
In the lamp bowl of the rose.
The golden Host is lifted high
In the monstrance of the sky,
And the world's perpetual shrine
Trembles with the living wine
Christ is risen! Earth is sweet
with the impress of His feet.[2]

The poem already shows the writing style that Caryll will continue to use: imagery from the natural world, opening onto a sense of eucharistic sacramentality, which in turn leads to strongly visual gospel images.

Further poems followed over the next few years. *The St. Leonards Chronicle* records the visits of Old Girls to the convent and school during these years, Caryll's name among them. It is likely that during this period the nuns at St. Leonards, and especially Mother Aloysia (with whom Caryll kept up a correspondence), were instrumental in her return to Catholicism.

In the meantime, she had to continue making a living. Around the mid-1920s, she began to put her art to work. She painted lampshades, made artificial roses, which she generally despised, and began doing regular work for Grossé, a church furnishings company that had originated in Belgium. This work began with a reredos for a Protestant church. She eventually became a lifelong friend of the company's owners, Elizabeth and Louis Billaux. She also became godmother to their son, David, as well as to Ruth and Dermot's older daughter, Deirdre.

In July 1923, a friend of Ruth's, Vivian Richardson, who rented a room in Gert's boardinghouse, introduced Caryll to a young woman named Iris Wyndham who had a two-year-old daughter named Joan. Iris was tall, striking, and sufficiently connected to high society to have been presented at court and to have had a coming-out ball. She was twenty-three years of age and unhappily married to Guy Richard Wyndham, known as Dick. Both Iris and her husband came from storied backgrounds. Iris's father was Percy Bennett, a distinguished British diplomat who had been a commercial attaché in various European cities in the late nineteenth century. In 1895 Percy was posted to Galatz, a town in Romania, where he met and married Winifred Youell, whose parents had moved there from England to pursue business interests, and whose beauty was admired throughout European society. Iris, born in Bucharest in 1900, was their only child. She was brought up in fashionable English boarding schools with the daughters of the wealthy and the titled. As a debutante, she had danced with the Prince of Wales on two occasions.

By the time Iris became an adult, her parents had long been amicably separated. Percy became the British ambassador to Panama and Costa Rica. Winifred was the mistress of Field Marshal John French, the commander-in-chief of the British Expeditionary Force during the first years of the Great War, and later the Lord Lieutenant of Ireland. On a visit to French in Dublin after the war, Winifred brought Iris with her. There, Iris met twenty-three-year-old Dick Wyndham, who was French's aide-de-camp. Iris and Dick were married in October 1920, and Joan was born the following year.

As for Dick himself, he was the grandson of Percy Scawen Wyndham, a Conservative Party politician, and his wife, Madeline, who had built a grand house known as "Clouds" in the late nineteenth century. Situated near the village of East Knoyle in Wiltshire, the sandstone and brick house was built according to an Arts and Crafts design, with furnishings by William Morris and other Pre-Raphaelite artists. The Wyndham couple had five children, and in addition to two nurseries, the house contained twenty-five bedrooms and airy reception rooms where weekend guests gathered. Glamorous parties were held, and guests such as

Oscar Wilde and Edward Burne-Jones provided clever and amusing conversation. Rooms opened up for dancing at night, and music floated out onto the terraces. The house was the center of a group of friends calling themselves The Souls, who held leisurely discussions about politics and ideas and conducted sexual affairs.

For two glittering decades the house hosted politicians, artists, and various grandees of the aristocracy and gentry. Then the revelry and lofty discussions came to a halt in August 1914 with the declaration of war against Germany. The grandchildren of Percy and Madeline Wyndham were now young adults, and six of their grandsons enlisted. Of the six, five were killed in combat over the four years of the war. Dick was the lone survivor and became the inheritor of Clouds.

By the time Caryll met her, Iris was the chatelaine of Clouds, by now a small glimmer of a house that had, at the height of its glory, hired about thirty servants. An attempt was made to maintain the prewar, leisure-class status of Clouds and its occupants. Iris wore expensive clothes and drove fancy cars. Her friends were equally endowed with privilege. She hosted hunting parties, noted in the visitor book the names of the couple's distinguished guests, and in the spirit of noblesse oblige, took charge of the Brownie troop in the nearby village. The marriage foundered, however, and the glamor of the house could not be maintained in the postwar world. The last entry recorded in the Clouds visitor book was the house party held in October 1922 to celebrate Joan's first birthday.

Upon meeting Caryll Houselander in 1923, Iris was fascinated not only with Caryll herself—her witty conversation and shabby appearance—but also with Caryll's lowlife surroundings: Gert's somewhat down-scale boardinghouse and coarse language and the drudgery of the household chores. The experience was unlike anything Iris had known before (having been, apparently, unaware of—and uninterested in—the lives of her own servants). She found herself visiting often, helping with the chores, attending Gert's parties in the spirit of *la nostalgie de la boue*.

Soon Iris asked Caryll if she could hire her to decorate her daughter's nursery, and then invited her to live at Clouds as she completed the job. The decorating work, a series of illustrations from fairy tales, took a week. There was little time to enjoy Caryll's handiwork, however: in November 1924, Iris obtained a divorce from Dick on the grounds of adultery. Her husband denied the allegation of adultery, but in order to hasten matters, he did the deed that was necessary at the time in order to obtain a divorce: he arranged to be caught in *flagrante delicto*. He wrote her a short letter: "Dear Iris, It is a long time since I have left you, and the longer I have been away the more do I realize that we are absolutely unfitted to one another. The enclosed bill will, therefore, be of interest to you. Yours, Dick."[3] The bill he referred to was from the Metropole Hotel in Brighton. It showed that the previous June he had been in a hotel room with a woman other than his wife (as in such cases of the era, he had likely hired a prostitute).

Now having to leave Clouds, Iris and Joan moved to a house in Bacombe Warren, near Wendover in Buckinghamshire. Iris brought a household with her: the cook, Kathleen; the housemaid, Winnie; the gardener, Brady; and Joan's nursemaid, Jessie. At some point she invited Caryll to live with them,[4] and the two would share a dwelling for the rest of Caryll's life. In 1925 they moved to London, where Iris rented a house at 28 Evelyn Gardens, South Kensington. Sir John French, Winifred's lover, died the same year, and Iris's mother, the disconsolate Winifred, known as Wendy (she and her lover had called each other "Peter Pan" and "Wendy") moved in with them. For a long time Wendy resented Caryll (she had expected that Iris would re-marry in the style she had become accustomed to, but by becoming interested in Catholicism as a result of Caryll's influence, her daughter was closing the door on that possibility). Two dogs and a tabby cat named Jones eventually rounded out the ménage. In this atmosphere, which had all the hallmarks of chaos, comedy, pathos, and high drama, Caryll pursued her search for God.

New Year's Eve party, 1925. From left at the table: Gert Houselander, Caryll, Iris Wyndham. Courtesy Camilla Shivarg.

Iris's upper-class friends did not know what to make of Caryll and her bohemian clothes and lower-class appearance. At times she was mistaken for a charwoman. A certain contempt was somewhat mutual: Caryll disdained the frivolous lives of the upper class. But when the frostiness between them began to thaw and they started engaging with one another, Iris's friends found Caryll to be a clever and amusing conversationalist. Around this time Caryll began telling people her name was Sidonie, and asked them to call her "Sid." This may have been a way of keeping Sidney Reilly's memory in her life, or she may have seen herself in the comedian Syd Walker, who played a Cockney music-hall rag-and-bone man, later popularized in the BBC radio program "Band Waggon" (although at one point during this period she also briefly called herself, for no discernible reason, "Yolande"). From earliest childhood, Joan knew her by both "Sid" and "Baby." Also during these years, Caryll began putting a white substance on her face. To some friends she explained that she did not like her ruddy complexion. Others thought that the crudely applied substance was a means of favoring her shyness, as if by covering her face she would somehow disappear from view. It may also have been a way of separating herself from Iris's world, even as remaining an integral part of it.

Some friends saw Caryll as Iris's hired live-in companion, and some assumed a form of lesbian arrangement. Indeed, after Caryll's death she and Iris would be casually described as "lesbians." Among their Catholic friends, it was assumed that they were simply two women friends sharing a home, as single women often did when husbands or boyfriends had been lost in the war. Although their friendship was a complex one (Caryll sometimes called Iris "Mother" and Caryll remained, at least for the first few years, "Baby"), Caryll's wholesale desire for dedication to God within the practice of the Catholic faith precluded anything beyond simple companionship.[5]

As their friendship was to deepen over the years, and they grew increasingly attached emotionally to one another, Iris and Caryll each seemed to offer the other something that was lacking in herself. The wealthy Iris, whose life had been superficial and loveless, and for whom marriage had produced a child but little else, found in Caryll a spiritual connection, and in her eventual conversion to Catholicism she found, like other converts, a religious structure and discipline for her life. For Caryll, living with Iris meant that she had a home and companionship as she tried to make sense of the spiritual turmoil inside herself. Many years later, she would write, "[T]hough in temperament we are so unlike, the friendship and love between us is like a rock, it is a thing we both do not cease to thank God for."[6]

In November 1925, Iris was baptized at the Servite Church, Our Lady of Dolours, having received instructions from the Italian-born Father Lothar Corato, a member of the Servite Order. Four-year-old Joan was also baptized. On December 8, Iris received her First Communion at St. Leonards. The Servite Church, the closest to where they lived, had become their parish church. Father Corato, who was thirty-nine when they first met him, had been a priest at the church for several years and would remain there for the rest of his life. He was quiet and unassuming, respected as a theologian, and known to be deeply prayerful. It is not known whether he ever became Caryll's confessor, but through the coming years he would spend many a lunch or supper at Caryll's table as part of her circle of friends.

It is unclear when Caryll met the two Jesuits who would become instrumental in her life. In early 1926, fifty-two-year-old Father Robert Steuart became the superior of the Jesuit community on Mount Street in the fashionable Mayfair district, which was attached to the Farm Street Church.[7] Father Steuart hailed from a family of Scottish Catholic aristocracy. As a young man he had gone into the army, where he proved to be reckless and wild in behavior and lazy in studies. A loud altercation with his father resulted in the angry retort, "I'll go and be a Jesuit!" "Not seriously," he later said, "but bitterly and unreflectively, as a man might say, 'I'll blow my brains out!' "[8] He had spent the whole four years of the war as a military chaplain in the trenches of France, and wrote movingly of his experiences there. After the war, nearly his whole priestly life was dedicated to writing, giving retreats, and helping people in spiritual direction. He was known to have a deep life of prayer, to have struggled with a tendency toward laziness as a young Jesuit, and he sometimes hinted at an inner "dark night" that was likely a form of depression. ("My pain, and the pain of all the world, is the Passion of Christ"[9] was a saying of Father Steuart's that Caryll would eventually make her own, and his writing on the mystical body of Christ would also be an influence.)

Caryll began going to Confession to Father Steuart. It is difficult to know how far his influence on her extended at this stage; in a notebook of this time, to which she gave the title "Spiritual Journal," she wrote: "To follow my confessor's advice without question or resentment in my heart. I think if I could only be more frank with my confessor all this would be easy, but unfortunately I am still too shy, and I think that such shyness comes either from pride or fear. I would very gladly trust him as if he were my father, but I feel it is almost impossible to let him know my heart, or let anyone know it but God."

Further on in her journal, she indicates that she has come to the conclusion that the writing she has done should join her artwork as a means of livelihood. "Up to now I have refused to let my writing enter my mind as a means of making money, but now I am deliberately doing all I can in this direction too. I expect my poems to be turned down everywhere and almost hope so. I am torn between the loathing of having even these torn to bits by my acquaintances and the knowledge that these also are talents for which God will one day inquire." She goes on: "I am preparing a set of old poems to submit, and as soon as they are out I will write some new ones, observing more care in regards to form." She adds: "I have applied for some sort of work in the line of illustration and children's poetry."[10]

This decision—to include her writing among the talents by which she might scrape out a living and to send out submissions to likely publications—probably led to one of the most important meetings in Caryll's life as a writer: a referral to the Jesuit Geoffrey Bliss, who was editor of the *Messenger of the Sacred Heart*. This publication was the magazine of the Apostleship of Prayer, a movement that had developed among Jesuits in France in the nineteenth century to foster devotion to the Sacred Heart. The devotion to the Heart of Jesus originated in medieval times, but had gained modern popularity in the seventeenth century when a Visitandine nun, St. Margaret Mary Alacoque, claimed to have visions in which Christ revealed to her his wish that his love be honored under the symbol of his heart. The devotion and the magazine were placed in the hands of the Jesuits.

When Caryll met Father Bliss for the first time, he had been editor of the magazine for six years and was contemplating a second magazine, one that would be geared toward children. This priest was in his early fifties, son of an Oxford scholar and clergyman who, through the influence of the Oxford Movement had followed John Henry Newman into the Catholic Church. His wife remained an Anglican but agreed that the children would be brought up Catholics and hoped that one son would dedicate his life to God.

As a Jesuit, Father Bliss spent years as a teacher before becoming editor of the *Messenger of the Sacred Heart* in 1920. As both a teacher and an editor, he was exacting, even vehemently so. A notice published after his death declared that "his voice was metallic, and in ordinary conversation often indistinct in utterance, while he had a disconcerting trick of spelling out the word a luckless hearer had failed to catch; his thinning hair looked frequently as if he had been grasping handfuls of it in exasperation, and he put on at times a wilfully misleading manner of abrupt incivility, accentuated by the grey gauntness of his cheeks."[11] His outward gruffness masked a sensitivity and courteousness and a deeply contemplative outlook. He was a man of letters and a lover of the arts, especially the poetry of his fellow Jesuit, Gerard Manley Hopkins.

The first of Caryll's poems—or "rhythms" as she and Father Bliss agreed to call them—appeared in the *Messenger* in 1927. These were followed by drawings and articles. In the early years, she kept a scrapbook of them all. Her name was affixed at the end of each article: usually "Frances Caryll Houselander," and occasionally "Frances C. Houselander." The scrapbook's cover had the title "Film Scrap Book for Your Favourite Stars," and it showed a smiling young woman holding scissors and glue. The language in the articles was concrete, engaging, and intimate, reflecting to some degree the floweriness of late Victorian literature ("When Mister Truffit was a young man he dug up all the little patch of ground around his cottage and made the soil good, and he built a low wooden fence about it. All this he took great pleasure in doing, for the sight of the red-brown soil was kind to his heart and the earth was wholesomeness and strength to him."[12]) There was always a reference to scripture that elevated the tone to the spiritual level with a takeaway for the reader. The concreteness and immediacy of the language suggests the influence of the Jesuit Spiritual Exercises, in which a person enters meditation by summoning up tangible details while contemplating certain gospel scenes. This vivid use of the five senses would become a feature in nearly all Caryll's writing.

In 1928, *The Children's Messenger* was inaugurated with Caryll's help. In the first issue, her drawings accompanied Father Bliss's commentary on the creed. *The Children's Messenger* was a monthly leaflet-sized periodical of about fifteen pages. The cover of each issue featured Caryll's drawing of the Christ child lying on a stylized manger, his arms extended. The drawing was enclosed in a circle, around which were the words THY KINGDOM COME. The first article of each issue was a commentary on the pope's intention within the Apostleship of Prayer for that month, written by Caryll. The language was limpid: short sentences (albeit with a literary appetite for semicolons), words of rarely more than two syllables, friendly but not too chatty: "The Pope tells us to pray for everybody to think that hard work is a fine and noble thing; and for everyone to work hard; and for everyone to think this, and do this, because of what religion teaches us. If you were a dog or a lion you wouldn't have to work. It's the same with plants: Jesus Christ said, 'The lilies of the field labour not, neither do they spin; but your heavenly Father feedeth them.' A man is much higher than an animal or a plant and yet he has to work. Why? Because he has the power of *thinking* and *planning* how to work, and strength to work with. God gave him these powers and God wants him to use them." Her rhetoric includes the question-answer method of a kindly teacher. Generally there is a Bible story told in Caryll's own words as well as a story, with a Christian moral to it, about contemporary boys and girls. Occasionally the commentary strays into the area of Catholic triumphalism ("The sheepfolds in this Pope's Intention are certain countries where most of the people are good Catholics and the Wolves (though they don't know they are wolves) are Protestant 'Missionaries' who try to entice the sheep out of the One Fold of the Catholic Church"), but as the years went on and Caryll's own spiritual horizons widened, such Catholic specialism declined. Concrete images were used to draw children into the stories ("Little Kurt pushed open the cottage door and ran out barefoot over the soft green grass"[13]). Caryll would be a mainstay in this work for the next decade and even beyond, and Father Bliss would be her champion until his death.

Caryll began her remarkable spiritual journal in 1925, and thus it predates, for the most part, her first meeting with Father Bliss. One can only assume that at the beginning any direct outside spiritual help would have come from her copious correspondence with Mother Aloysia and aid from Father Steuart in confession. The journal makes many references to her tendency toward laziness and a need for a solid timetable in her day. She sets down a disciplined schedule for herself: to plan her day the evening before; to set a time for her work that allows time for Mass, private prayer, and spiritual reading; to be self-controlled in her times of relaxation.

Several more directives continue. Her tone becomes penitential, as if she is a nun in an austere cloister ("Never to waste God's time interiorly, that is never to cease praying for a second"; "to offer every motion separately to God, by a simple little intention"; "to work standing, unless really very tired or ill"; "always to sit up straight, never to lean back, this even if I am tired"; "to praise God whenever I am conscious of discomfort"; "to kneel on bare board when making acts of contrition"). In spite of herself, worldliness breaks in upon the austerity with the determined plan "not to smoke more than ten cigarettes a day," but then to top off her daily plan, she adds a list called "Special Rules to Aid Charity":

1. Punctuality at meals, care not to keep people waiting
2. To see Christ in every one, never to show the least annoyance when inconvenienced by people, always to be gentle and say in my heart, "It is you, Lord."
3. Always to include others in my prayers for myself
4. Not to suggest things I would like to do
5. Not to ask people to sit with me

6. Not to talk of Art or to seek sympathy
7. Never to complain or grumble
8. To suffer fools gladly!
9. To seek obscurity always (n.b. not to drink when I am thirsty)
10. To pray for sinners at night
11. To be silent whenever I can without being too obvious.

Then, as if floundering to find a way to love God and to experience God's love for her, she seems to consider the lives of the saints, in particular the medieval women saints. She mimics their language of visions and direct communication with God. "I think Our Lord asks me to get up and pray every night this winter even if it is very cold and to beg His mercy for sinners," she writes, looking to bodily penance as the best means to do the will of God. "Presently I thought that the Cross was in front of me"—and she goes on to visualize Christ in pain, shedding blood for abandoned sinners. St. Thérèse of the Child Jesus, having died at the age of twenty-four and having been canonized only in 1925, was surely on her mind when she wrote: "I must be at pains to do everything, however small, thoroughly and completely, and so through little things to die completely to myself."

After expounding on her visions, she comes down to earth by addressing her need to make a livelihood. The rest of her journal, with the exception of a series of passages describing a trip to Wiesbaden in Germany—which she took with her former fiancé's mother,[14] and in which worldly delights take over for a sentence in the form of gifts to take home ("some china dogs and bears, a doll, a toy cat and some sausages to give to my friends")—is taken up primarily with her need for God and, especially, her faults. These consist mainly of her tendency to speak unkindly of others, her laziness, and inability to curtail her cigarette habit. "The spirit of criticism in me is a great hindrance to the grace of God," she writes. "I ought to be bitterly ashamed in considering that I often criticize God's priests in just the same way that the Pharisees criticized Our Blessed Lord." And elsewhere: "Tobacco! What a thing to put before God."

Her inability to pray plagues her: "I so badly want to pray always. I want to pray with my heart and soul and body, to make not many but one unceasing act of love." She speaks of being constantly tired and ill with unspecified bodily ailments, and despite these physical setbacks no one pities her. "When I say unkind things it is nearly always because I imagine that no one cares for me," she writes. "How ungrateful this is in one who being born with no claim on any one, has been fed and clothed and educated and who has been taken in and protected again and again, having nothing to give in return."

She scours the gospels for clues to her own spiritual life, comparing herself to St. Peter and others. "St. Peter, dear saint of impulses, pray for me that I may stop cutting off people's ears." Elsewhere she accuses herself of casting the first stone, just for the fun of it. Then she writes, "I have ceased to expect anything of myself and it is happier so. Somehow, so long as one expects anything of oneself, one remains at the centre of one's life: every failure means bitter and often wasted sadness. . . . Now I expect nothing of myself, just nothing at all, or of anyone else: the result is I expect everything of God." Without much pause, she then continues to expect much of herself.

During the time period of this journal, she seems to rely on *The Imitation of Christ* by Thomas à Kempis and the anonymously written *The Cloud of Unknowing*. The journal reads as if she wants to live an intense Christian spiritual life in a way that nuns live, but without the benefit of a community or cloister or a vowed way of life. She makes resolutions and calls them "my rule of life," as if modeling herself after a medieval anchoress. This "rule of life" consumes her, and again, a daily regimen is outlined. Get up at once in the morning, go to bed early, say set prayers at certain times of the day, go to Mass at the same time every day, begin work promptly.

Her poverty bothers her and gets in the way of her spiritual life: "not having no money, but having no paint to earn it with, no bus fares to go to fetch the work, no materials to make samples, every side hampered, every way shut off and sneers and comments on my debts from the very person who has deprived me of my own money!" This may have been a slam at her mother; friends said after Caryll's death that Gert kept the money that Willmott sent for Caryll's use. Debts that she owed to unspecified partners in disastrous business forays also weigh her down. One of these partners was charged with fraud and tried at the Old Bailey. Another venture was the failed attempt with a man named Frost to set up a small shop to sell her carvings. Caryll does not include in her journal her distress at the bailiff's appearance at Evelyn Gardens or her amusement at Frost's unusual way with mispronunciations: for years, she would mimic his pronunciation of "unique and bizarre" as "uni-cue and bizzery."[15]

As an almost last-ditch attempt at scaling the heights of charity, she examines the lives of people around her and tries to learn from their virtues: "[F]rom Iris, not to talk too much, to be tolerant, from Miss Bishop [who had been hired as a governess for Joan], not to be critical of religious things, more reverence for priests. From Jessie, to get up more promptly, not to be ashamed of letting my efforts be seen. From Kathleen, true humility. From Mrs. Henan, patience in matters of poverty, pleasure in seeing others better off." She is a waif in the wilderness, wanting to soar in love of God, blocked in some ways by her vast needs and imperfections.

By the end of 1927, she reminds herself, like someone who is mature in the spiritual life, that "the interior life of poverty is what counts." She adds, "It is through that, that I shall learn detachment: to be ignored by Iris's friends; to let them take her away for long intervals, giving her the pleasures that I cannot give her; to be aware that they attribute to me only the basest motives for remaining with her and neither to resent it or to be bitter; to learn not to complain, even to God." Then, in an indication of the tug-of-war she would have with money for the rest of her life, she writes: "In a way, since I only am humiliated by it, I prefer to live on charity than in any other way, for I think there is no other life so utterly humiliating, not only in the eyes of others but of myself." There is no record of any payment given to Caryll for her work with Father Bliss, and it is possible that she worked for nothing. It may be that she accepted no payment from Grossé as well.

On March 13, 1928, she writes that she has been received "as a novice of the Third Order of St. Francis." Nothing more is known of this step or of the influence that led her to take it. It may have been a step toward giving some structure to her desire for evangelical poverty: members of the Third Order lived "in the world" as seculars, rather than in a monastery or religious house and rather than taking vows, they made solemn promises to live according to the spirit of St. Francis. Although Caryll had always proven in one way or another that she did not easily fit into any group, she may have felt the need for guidance in living, like St. Francis, a life of poverty while suffering through her endless cycle of self-criticism and longing for God.

By the following July, she gives her problem the name of "creatures" (probably a term picked up from *The Imitation of Christ*)—people and things that in one way or another keep her from loving God more perfectly. At the top of the list is "Iris," and the list includes "Spending of money," "Words," "Iris's friends," and "Joan." The presence of Iris and Joan under the category of "creatures" indicates an ongoing tension in the household. Does she see Joan as a rival?

Years later, recalling the period when she was trying to beat her faults out of herself, she wrote that she "tried (quite literally) to flog this devil that could hate and condemn out of myself. I made up my mind that when I saw something which I condemned in others, I would punish myself for it. I would be flogged and starved for them. There were two results: first I realized how very censorious I must really be, for I was one bruise from head to foot (or at least so far as the covered parts of me went), and secondly I was in danger of starving to death, though being obviously hysterical, I could go three days without food. But there was another result, less ludicrous. I got an amazing tenderness for the people I was doing it for."[16]

Caryll may be exaggerating in this description of medieval self-torture that indicates a total concentration on her own imperfection and no allowance for God's mercy. Neither of the two Jesuits in her life would have condoned such self-punishment. Father Steuart, in particular, preached gentleness and common sense in the spiritual life. All indications are, however, that the seesaw of eating and not-eating would be a matter of concern, at least from time to time, throughout her life.

On January 20, 1929, she refers to an eight-month gap in her journal between that date and the previous July. Smoky, the London barrister and friend of her youth, had died in that interval, on September 4, 1928. She writes, perhaps a bit melodramatically: "Now the old conquests have given place to a slow crucifixion of the heart. . . . Day after day brings the thought of Smoky deeper into my heart. I am happy for him and long to die to be with him again."

The extant part of the spiritual journal ends on March 7, 1929, as it begins, in self-castigation: "I am as unkind as before, my tongue as violent, my mind as melancholy, my self-indulgence grown as I could never have imagined, my spirit of prayer fading." She writes that she will perform more "practices" ("excepting those which proved impractical"). She will allow herself "the luxury of lying at His feet in silence, not even looking up: just knowing that He is there, His hand above my head." She quotes from the last lines of Francis Thompson's poem, "The Hound of Heaven": "That Voice is round me like a bursting sea."[17]

With the 1930s ahead, Caryll, approaching thirty herself, living on Iris's largesse and surrounded by the shabbiness of her own life, remained unsure of where that Voice was leading her. Her artistic talents were now being realized in the making of crucifixes, statues, and Stations of the Cross for Grossé. And not far ahead was a new friend who would have a huge influence on her life as a writer.

4

Calm Leading
to Storm Threat
(1930–1939)

Realization of our oneness in Christ is the only cure for human loneliness. For me, too, it is the only ultimate meaning of life, the only thing that gives meaning and purpose to every life.

—A Rocking-Horse Catholic

By the time of her thirtieth birthday, Caryll had landed on her feet with a home at Evelyn Gardens, regular work, and, at the top of the house, a room of her own that doubled as an art studio. Iris made all the decisions regarding the household and, still inclined to a life of luxury, she maintained to some extent her former style, keeping an elegant paneled drawing room and beautiful ornate furniture, and maintaining contact with her upper-class friends. She paid all the household expenses, and Caryll was left free to pursue her work for Grossé and Father Bliss, who ran his periodicals from his office in Wimbledon, on the grounds of Sacred Heart Church, which at the time was served by Jesuits. Caryll refused to allow friends to pay her for the art she did for them. The Servite Church, where she went to Mass each morning, continued to be her parish church. No further journal of her inner spiritual struggles survives, but it is possible that she chose to work without pay in her continuing desire to be poor.

Physically, Caryll was slight and when standing next to the statuesque Iris, came no further than her friend's shoulder. She had blue-green eyes, generally hidden behind thick glasses so that a person did not know if she was or was not looking at them when she spoke. The bangs on her forehead stopped at the top of her glasses, and when she bent over to work, her hair, shiny and carrot-colored, fell like a curtain along the side of her face. The white powder on her face gave her a grotesque look that was accentuated by perspiration and a yellow-brown cigarette streak that slid from the corner of her mouth to her chin. She did not like to show her teeth, possibly because they had rarely been attended to by a dentist and had become discolored.[1] Many years later she would write to a friend that she was "self-conscious" about her looks.[2] She had small hands, which were usually kept busy with a chisel and hammer or carving knife. She was precise and workmanlike in her art, took meticulous care of her tools, and kept her living spaces clean and tidy, with no clutter.

As Caryll matured, friends were aware of a "second sight," or psychic ability in her. She spoke of experiences that would corroborate this perception, but it was never known whether Caryll was accurate in telling stories of what had happened to her, or whether they were simply tall tales that she was having fun with. She did have extraordinary insight, however, which some described as a natural clairvoyance. This natural gift would become evident in the years to come when people came to her for help as a result of her published work. She had learned handwriting analysis from a manual as an art student, and fellow students had pressed her to "read" their handwriting. She continued studying it, keeping books and newspaper cuttings on the subject, and friends enjoyed it when she continued the practice as a parlor game.[3]

Her parents resurfaced in her life, though her mother had never been far away. At some point, Gert, the sports enthusiast, had acquired a motorcycle, and she appeared regularly at Evelyn Gardens, loud and brash, wearing trousers and a leather outfit and helmet. Friends later remembered that she also drove a taxi-like vehicle at times. She could also be moody and was capable of ruining a gathering of friends by simply sitting and glowering. When she was in a good mood, Gert and Caryll engaged in bantering back and forth, egging each other on, both having a quick mind and the gift of repartee. Willmott Houselander acquired a yacht, and Caryll sometimes brought her friends sailing with him. He retired from his banking profession in 1934 and settled in London in a style equal in eccentricity to that of his estranged wife and his daughter, having acquired a parrot and hired a maid named Elsie, who had only one leg and who managed, in spite of this disability, to keep house for him on crutches. With Willmott's move to London, the estranged couple, who had never divorced, kept up an affectionate hostility toward each other, often sharing household help and keeping in touch in the face of each other's needs. Both parents used vulgar language, which Caryll did as well, having picked it up at home from earliest years.

The presence of Joan, Iris's young daughter, in the household provided an unaccustomed touch of childhood in Caryll's life. Caryll decorated the nursery in the same kind of fairyland whimsy that she had done in the nursery at Clouds and used Joan as a model when she illustrated stories for *The Children's Messenger*. As they established themselves as a household, Caryll tended to admonish Iris for spoiling the child. Joan herself was somewhat scared of Caryll, and also fascinated by her: her wild appearance, the cigarette that dangled from her mouth, and in later years, her penetrating and otherworldly intelligence. Caryll invited unusual friends to visit and brought home books that covered a wide range of interest that Joan, as she grew older, delved into. Caryll gave her informal lessons in wood carving and painting, and Joan found that she wanted Caryll's approval. When she was seven, Joan was sent as a weekly boarder to the Convent of the Assumption, not far from their home, and a few years later, to Caryll's old school at St. Leonards.[4]

In July 1932, another important person in Caryll's writing life arrived in London. She was a twenty-nine-year-old Dutch woman called Baroness Yvonne Bosch van Drakestein, whose family's Catholic aristocratic roots stretched back to medieval Europe. Yvonne wore the smart dress of a contemporary businesswoman and belonged to a group called Women of Nazareth, which had been founded eleven years earlier by a Dutch Jesuit by the name of Jacques van Ginneken. This group was one of several new movements that had come about as a new social order was being built in the wake of the 1914–18 war. These new movements emerged under the general umbrella of "Catholic Action." The idea was to make use of sacred tradition and the sacramental life of the Church to revitalize society toward a renewal of Christian culture beyond a fortress-style defense of Catholicism. Father van Ginneken, a philologist by training, envisioned a new way for Catholic laity to live a dedicated Christian life and to bring the Gospel to the modern world by contemporary means. To give concrete expression to this idea, he founded four lay communities, each intended to concentrate on a specific group of people: the Ladies of Bethany, the Knights of St. Willibrord, and in 1921, the Crusaders of St. John and the Women of Nazareth.

With the breakdown of the old order and the rise of Communism, Father van Ginneken foresaw women as a powerful influence outside the domestic arena, a potential to be tapped. The Ladies of Bethany would eventually become a religious order, but his plan for the Women of Nazareth was that they would dedicate their lives to doing important Christian work in the world. They would make simple promises similar to vows, but would wear secular clothing rather than religious habits, and would not live within convent walls. Over the next few years, the purpose of the Women of Nazareth evolved from the conversion of non-Catholic girls to a focus on young Catholic women in an effort to help them deepen their spiritual lives in the face of sweeping secularization.

Yvonne had been studying the history of art in Nijmegen when a friend introduced her to Father van Ginneken, who was lecturing at the university. She worked as an assistant for him and before long became a member of the Women of Nazareth. She was sent to work in a chocolate factory in order to have experience with women of the working class. She displayed leadership qualities and remarkable physical stamina, and was soon sent to Java (present-day Indonesia), and had hardly arrived there when she was told to leave for England. The purpose in Yvonne's arrival in London was to form an English branch of the movement.

In Europe, the rising tide of political movements favored the use of huge military-style marches accompanied by an emphasis on efficiency and order, and these became a model for the new Catholic women's organization. In Amsterdam, the Women of Nazareth put on huge processions and rallies with enormous banners and thousands of participants wearing colorful uniforms. The uniforms consisted of skirts, blouses, and berets, and sometimes cloaks, which varied in color according to one's rank within the organization. The ranks were also determined by the class system of the time, the highest ranks taken by members of the aristocracy.

The idea behind the wearing of a uniform at these outsized events was that one's individuality was overshadowed by becoming part of a movement much larger than oneself—a contrast to the individualism in the rest of society. The wearing of a uniform also made clear to the outside world that the members wearing it were part of a community that stood for something. The result was a youthful female army that showed a renewed devotion to Christianity and in particular, to Catholicism. In Amsterdam, these events reached their pinnacle in 1932 in the stadium built for the 1928 summer Olympics, when ten thousand girls and young women performed a choreographed pageant based on the Pentecost sequence, *Veni Sancte Spiritus* ("Come, Holy Spirit"). Around this time, the Women of Nazareth became known as Ladies of the Grail, named after the rich symbolism contained in the medieval legend of the cup Jesus used at the Last Supper.

Soon after her arrival in London, Yvonne Bosch van Drakestein met with Cardinal Francis Bourne, the archbishop of the West-minster Archdiocese, who invited her to set up a Grail chapter in England at once. A house on Sloane Street was rented as head-quarters, and the Grail in England began under the direction of Yvonne, who much later would be described as "a strong leader, far-sighted and inspirational, if at times a little autocratic."[5] In 1933 the Grail performed the spectacular *Everyman* in the Royal Albert Hall in London, with five hundred people taking part. A magazine called *Fire* (later changed to *The Grail*) was begun, with Yvonne as editor. The same year, Cardinal Bourne lent the Grail a house at Eastcote, just outside London, to train young English women. Spiritual campaigns and training weekends were held in parishes, bringing a fresh Christian spirit to the youth. In 1936 another spectacle, based on Francis Thompson's "The Hound of Heaven," took place at the Royal Albert Hall, with twelve hundred young women performing.

It was inevitable that, given the splash of the Grail's arrival within Catholic London, Caryll Houselander's interest would be piqued. Four decades later, Yvonne, in her old age, would recall her first meeting with Caryll at the Grail House on Sloane Street:

> One day somebody rang the bell. I answered the door, and on the doorstep was what I thought was a girl, small and thin, with red hair cut straight, with a straight fringe. Her hair was carrot-red, and she had green eyes and white eyelashes! She looked a bit like a clown. She asked if she could see the head of the Grail. I said, "I am." She looked rather surprised and came in. She carried a small, longish box, and she said, "I hear you have come to England, and I want to help you because I hear you are very keen on banners, and I am in a kind of trade where we make church furnishings, and I brought you a little banner in case you would be interested." She opened the box, and out came a little felt banner embroidered with gold in the old traditional way, with gold fringes.

Yvonne went on to explain to Caryll that for their processions the Grail used enormous stiff banners that were four or five yards long and three yards wide: " 'The young people of the world are not so terribly keen on walking with a little banner in the church anymore, at least in Holland they aren't.' So Caryll laughed her head off. She said, 'I only had this as an excuse to have an entry into the Grail.' "[6]

After the initial surprise of Caryll's appearance, Yvonne found a highly creative artist in her, and Caryll soon put her gifts to the service of the Grail, painting backdrops for the spectacles and carving a set of Stations of the Cross for the Sloane Street chapel. Yvonne, who edited *The Grail*, eventually took Caryll on as an artist and later as a writer. Caryll herself refused payment for the work she produced.

During these years of the early 1930s, a number of factors, besides the coming of Yvonne and the Grail to London, converged to add spark to Caryll's spiritual life. Caryll would soon use Yvonne as a sounding board as her creativity blossomed. She also had the influence of Father Bliss and Father Steuart (years later, writing to a correspondent who was looking for spiritual help, she recommended, among others, "all the books of Father R.H.J. Steuart, S.J.").[7] She was continuing to teach herself the fundamentals of the Christian spiritual life by reading the classics, including *Revelations of Divine Love*, by fourteenth-century anchoress Julian of Norwich. In this volume, Julian, suffering from severe illness, had a series of "showings" of the Passion of Christ. A 1933 issue of the periodical *New Blackfriars* published an article by Father Steuart called "Mother Julian of Norwich." The first paragraph of the article is a primer for what Caryll would eventually take as her own: "Holiness is one thing only, the Christ-life," Father Steuart writes, citing St. Paul's letter to the Galatians: "I live now not I, but Christ lives in me." He goes on to say that by Baptism believers "are to equate their lives to His, putting Him on, being formed into Him." He explains further: "It is more than just modelling themselves upon the precepts that He has given: by this mystical incorporation with Him there is planted in their being a Christ-germ which is the life of their life."[8]

Father Steuart's writerly tendency to create hyphenated double-words ("Christ-germ") and to turn a noun into a verb by adding the active -ing form would become Caryll's as well. "Christ-ing," he writes elsewhere, leaning toward an understanding of Christ in such a way that in the suffering of each Christian, it is Christ who suffers. And in a later letter to Yvonne, Caryll refers to their common "Christhood," "Christ-life," and, like Father Steuart, "the Christing of the world."[9] Indeed, this is a verbal practice (as well as a central teaching) that comes from Julian herself, and Father Steuart quotes her: "I saw a great one-ing betwixt Christ and us, for when He was in pain we were in pain."[10] In a further article on Julian, Father Steuart again quotes the anchoress, indicating that his idea of Christ-in-us is in fact taken from her teaching: "I understood that we be now, in Our Lord's meaning, in His Cross with Him in our pains and our Passion, dying."[11]

The teaching of the mystical body of Christ, with roots in the New Testament, would, over the following years, become Caryll's passion and would absorb her thoughts and much of her writing. At first she considered the mystical body as including only those baptized in the Catholic Church, but as her experiences widened, she would seek to include Jews, and in fact, all the human race. In an undated letter to a man with whom she had a mutual interest in Russian matters (including Russian refugees), she wrote regarding Christ's Passion as lived in the suffering of Christians: "On the other hand, if His beauty seems at times almost hidden in what we see of Christians . . . it is also revealed vividly over and over again where one least expects it in what I call 'Unconscious Christs' and in people who are not considered respectable by the world."[12]

In a long 1935 letter to Elizabeth Billaux, who had questions concerning an article Caryll had written, Caryll attempted to elucidate a question of Elizabeth's, "about man seeing God in other men." "I am not a theologian and not very well fitted to expound on Doctrine," Caryll wrote, "but as I understand it, the doctrine is this: that in every baptised Christian (which means anyone baptised at all, not only those baptised by a Catholic priest, and includes those who have the baptism of desire and of blood)—in the soul of every baptised Christian Christ lives. He is, as it were, a germ of Christ in them, or a seed of Christ. This seed of Christ grows and flowers in them as they correspond to grace and the whole object of a Christian is to become 'another Christ.' "[13] This was probably not the first time that Caryll used letters to friends in order to work out her understanding of the Christian life, nor would it be her last.

Caryll continued painting and carving for friends during this period. One such carving was a Byzantine eight-pointed cross for the Society of St. John Chrysostom, signaling an ongoing interest in the beauty of Russian liturgies, which had been an abiding inclination ever since she had crawled her way back to the Catholic Church (and it may also have been a way of maintaining a lingering attachment to the memory of Sidney Reilly). She continued to be attracted to the Russian Orthodox spiritual tradition. The Jesus prayer was a favorite because of the sense it gave of zeroing in on the one thing necessary. One of her favorite books was *Flame in the Snow*, the story of the Russian St. Seraphim of Sarov, a late eighteenth- and early nineteenth-century monk who lived a life of asceticism in a forest hut and preached a simple devotion to Jesus.

Her visual art had become central to her life during these years. A news account in the *St. Leonards Chronicler*, the annual magazine of the school, relates: "Caryll Houselander has turned all her artistic gifts to great account. She now makes wondrous painted crucifixes and statues, Stations of the Cross, besides using her pen and pencil in the service of God. Her unusual designs met with great favour."[14] A few years later, *The Pylon*, the missionary magazine of the Sisters of the Holy Child Jesus, described the results of her carving:

> Miss Houselander's Stations of the Cross are inspired by artistic ideals worthy of special mention. She deliberately departs from any purely historical or "realistic" representation of the

events of the Passion and gives us a symbol of some aspect of it, such as may enter into the life of any individual. In her composition she shuns distracting detail, and uses line as the simplest means of expression. Lines infallibly convey suggestions to the mind: thus descending and curving downwards they convey sorrow; short and rising they convey joy, and a circle gives a sense of infinite completeness. The artist's second means of expression lies in the use of rhythm or repetition of movement. Her forms are simple to the verge of austerity and her language is as that of a child. Her drawings rank among those that grow in depth and significance as they grow in familiarity.[15]

Caryll's circle of friends continued to grow as people joined them who had become Catholics through Caryll's influence. She told wildly entertaining stories and enjoyed racy jokes. Caryll and Iris learned to play the ukulele, and they put on evening concerts with friends who played the piano. Sometimes Caryll banged on a drum. She also shared to a small degree Iris's high-class life, accompanying her at times to the opera and theater. She was a delight at parties, capable of raucous laughter and able to tell salty stories using the same language that her father had used from the time she had been a small child. Gin flowed at the parties (a favorite gin drink for both Caryll and Iris was "white lady"). Caryll was never satisfied with one drink, and after a few her natural gift for mimicry and repartee tended to disintegrate into unkind remarks, which led to sober remorse. This tendency to make cutting comments about others after a few drinks would remain with her, as would her contriteness. But close friends would be aware that as the years went on, Caryll's inner bohemian party girl would begin to fuse seamlessly with her profound sense of God's presence in her life.

She was scathing in her criticism of certain aspects of Catholicism, tending to be critical of priests and nuns. Using fake Latin, she and her friends liked to imitate the way some priests said Mass. For Caryll, this mockery may have partly been the result of a dawning realization that reverence and awe were the necessary attitudes to bear upon sacred rituals. As for nuns, she would always remember her experience of the nuns' attitude at St. Leonards, where she had observed that girls from "respectable" families were sometimes treated differently than other girls. Despite her friendship with Mother Aloysia and the help she had received from her, as well as the enthusiasm with which she continued to be embraced at St. Leonards after her leave-taking, the sense of having been made to feel inferior at one time infuriated her. She would refer in later years to the "caste" system within the Church and the attitude of "fashionable" nuns: "It isn't the Catholic attitude but the attitude of the rich, protected child of the rich, protected parents that is disastrous,"[16] she wrote in a later undated letter. She admired the Salvation Army, especially after reading a biography of Bramwell Booth, the Army's first chief of staff, because of their care for the poor and outcast of society and their refusal to pander to respectability.[17]

Even as she continued to move deeper into her understanding of the Christian spiritual life, her speech remained unrefined. She tried to curtail her use of the epithet "bloody," knowing that some of her friends disapproved of it. Her most-used expression, however, one that her friends would always remember, was "buggered up a gum tree,"[18] the phrase she habitually used to describe her state of mind when confronted with a problem.

Iris's mother Wendy's extravagant and exotic wardrobe from her days as a paramour was a source of fun, and among the friends, there was a good deal of dressing up in gowns and furs. On one bizarre occasion, Caryll wore Wendy's curly golden wig to go to Mass at the Farm Street Church in the upscale Mayfair area of London, along with one of Wendy's outsized capes. Ostensibly, she told friends that she did not want to be recognized by acquaintances who went to that church, but wearing such an outrageous costume may have also been an attempt to thumb her nose at the parishioners who might otherwise not consider her to be a suitable presence. It was one of Caryll's strange eccentricities that, even as her theological understanding became more sophisticated and her spiritual life deepened, there remained an outward outlandishness about her during this time.

At Christmastime, the friends put on a pantomime, the silly and popular English entertainment for that time of year. They chose to perform *Aladdin*, with Caryll writing the script ("What ho, my naughty boy Aladdin. I'll smack your bottom without paddin' "[19]). A new convert named Henry Tayler, who was to become one of Caryll's best friends, played the empress with Wendy's curly wig and one of her shimmering gowns. The star of the show was Gert, perhaps an actress manquée, who brought the house down by playing the genie of the lamp. Birthdays were another occasion for high celebration. Caryll loved birthdays: the anticipation and whisperings in the lead-up to the big day, the excitement and fuss of the birthday itself, which was always celebrated with some kind of ritual—flowers, cake and candles on the table, and lots of presents, mostly inexpensive, but wrapped with a colorful riot of ribbons and bows.

Mock ballet at the Settlement House in Poplar, east-end London. From the left at the back: Jacques Doneux (a member of the Grossé staff), Caryll, Elizabeth Billaux, Iris Wyndham. The two women in the front are unknown. Courtesy Camilla Shivarg.

Another show some of the group performed took place at a Settlement center in Poplar, one of the poorest sections of London at the time. The center was a house of hospitality under the aegis of the Society of the Holy Child Jesus, where the friends went to volunteer. An entertainment craze carried over from the nineteenth century was for tableaux, and in the tableau spirit, Caryll and her friends performed a mock ballet, a spectacle that was all tutus and awkward legs and clumsy bodies. In her diary, Joan, who was now a young teenager, described the theatrical effort as cringe-worthy. She went off in a fit of embarrassed giggles at the sight of Iris, her long-legged, bespectacled mother as she tried to unfold like a rose and tripped over herself in her tiny pink tutu.[20]

The mid-1930s brought changes. Iris's grand-dame style had diminished, and in 1935 the household, fewer in number, moved to 7 Milborne Grove, still in the same part of London. The property had a small potting shed in the back garden, and for the remainder of the time they lived there, this shed became Caryll's studio. It also served as a tiny home-within-a-home, with Caryll hosting suppers as well as doing her carving there. The furnishing was sparse, with two chairs and a table as well as a cupboard and a workbench. The shed was uninsulated, and a paraffin stove heated it in the winter. She kept the shed meticulously tidy, and her art materials clean and well cared for.

In 1936, Caryll saw her name on the front cover of a book for the first time. *A Retreat with Saint Ignatius: In Pictures for Children* was published by Sheed & Ward. The text was by Father Bliss, and "F. Caryll Houselander" was named as the illustrator. The book contained rather intricate and elaborate illustrations, unlike the simple lines of her usual work, and the text, while well-meaning, was uninspiring. Still, she was pleased with her accomplishment, inscribing a copy to her godson, David Billaux, the son of Louis and Elizabeth Billaux: "In the first year of his life, my first published book."

The same year, Wendy, Iris's mother, died. After a decade of fighting the advancing years with beauty treatments and slimming machines and resenting Caryll for Iris's conversion to Catholicism, she had become gentle and calm on her deathbed. Before lapsing into semi-consciousness and uttering rambling phrases in her native Romanian, Wendy asked for Caryll to be with her.

About two years later, Caryll's vulgar side emerged when she and Joan visited Wendy's grave. According to Joan's diary/memoir, the two "made jokes in the worst possible taste all the way there in the train and became hysterical with laughter when we couldn't find the grave." They played a kind of hide-and-seek among the gravestones, and when they finally found Wendy's grave, Caryll "behaved very badly at the graveside and we had a hard job keeping on our faces of gloom in front of the sexton."[21]

During these years Caryll and a group of friends—at the beginning the group consisted of Elizabeth and Louis Billaux and others connected to Grossé—put their Christian zeal to practical use by forming a group called "Loaves and Fishes" (named after the miracle in the gospel, in which Jesus multiplied a small donation of loaves and fishes in order to feed a multitude). The idea was to help people who had fallen on hard times and were near destitution but were unable to find work and too ashamed to ask for charity. Everyone involved in the enterprise was given a fish name. The people in need were called "Sea-horses," and the person in overall charge was known as the "Red Herring." The people who agreed to help them anonymously were known as "Sprats," and each Sprat paid a pound a month into the common purse, of which Iris was in charge. Part of the Sprats' work was to engage the financial help of rich people, who were known as "Mackerels." A spare bedroom at the top of the house on Milborne Grove was used as the group's headquarters. Father Corato, of the Servite Church, known to the group as the "Holy Halibut," served as the Sprats' chaplain. "All must have one spirit," Caryll wrote in a small notebook where she explained the policies of the group. "The chilling attitude of 'good works' must be anathema, and in order that the completely personal and individual nature of the work be preserved there can only be the minimum 'organization' possible."[22]

As the 1930s wore on, Caryll's influence within *The Grail* was noticeable, although, at her own insistence, she wrote without pay. A piece called "What Is the Missionary Spirit?" bears the unmistakable sign of Caryll's handprint (and was later acknowledged to have been written by Caryll): the simple sentences, the direct phrasing, the lead-up to a final, crucial statement that, given Father Steuart's influence,[23] marks the central motif of Caryll's thinking about the Church:

> The Church is not, as we are prone to think, simply the hierarchy; it is not the Pope, the Cardinals, the priests and nuns and the Cathedrals of the world. Those things are part of the Church, but equally essential, equally the Church are we, ourselves, and the responsibility which is the cross laid upon the shoulders of the Pope, is equally the responsibility of each one of us without exception. . . . We depend upon each other, we are responsible for one another, and our communion with each other, our oneness is nothing less than Christ on earth. We are the mystical body of Christ, we are the utterance of Christ today.[24]

By the late 1930s, rumblings on the other side of the English Channel could not be ignored. Gas masks had already appeared, and the British government had issued precautions against the possibility of air raids. In 1938, Caryll and Iris joined the Volunteer Aid Detachment, which taught volunteers how to do rudimentary first-aid treatments, such as cleansing and bandaging wounds, and splinting broken bones. They took part in morale-boosting activities which gave practical advice on how to act when under attack. Month-by-month, tension rose as the question of "war" or "peace" hung in the balance across the nation while the prime minister, Neville Chamberlain, sought appeasement with Hitler. On September 29, Caryll's thirty-seventh birthday, Joan, who had finished school and was now studying acting, wrote in her diary that "Darling Chamberlain has gone to see Hitler,"[25] and the newspapers were now declaring peace. Caryll, Iris, and Joan, limp with relief, went to a Mass of thanksgiving at Westminster Cathedral and then "had a riotous birthday breakfast with pâté de foie, candles and gramophone records, and piles of presents and flowers to celebrate."[26]

The relief did not last long. In 1939, Yvonne Bosch van Drakes-tein moved to the Grail house in Eastcote for safety reasons. As a result, a series of letters to Yvonne from Caryll remain because of the necessity of writing her thoughts to her friends rather than speaking them in person or over the telephone. The letters reveal the deep attachment to Yvonne that Caryll had formed over the past few years. They indicate an ease in sorting out in words the jumbled spiritual thoughts that had been percolating within her, and they also reveal Caryll's need for what she felt was a strong motherly presence in Yvonne (although Yvonne was two years younger than Caryll). Whether she was expressing a latent sexual attraction in the letters or using the language of love to express a childlike enthusiasm is not known. She often wrote in enthusiastic terms whenever she thanked someone for a gift or expressed joy at the prospect of seeing them again. Then, too, the day-to-day existence of people in London as they awaited a war that never seemed to arrive caused considerably high tension.

Caryll, living in apprehension of what was coming next, seemed to be using an overabundance of language and an overly effusive choice of words as her creativity bubbled up in the letters to Yvonne. The groping toward an understanding of the coming suffering is an important aspect of how Caryll sees the world around her in these letters, and she stretches herself to express it. Nearly all of Caryll's letters to Yvonne during this period refer to her correspondent as *nmùrka*, a Russian term of endearment with the approximate meaning of "little bird."

Caryll feared the approach of war, and in the first extant letter to Yvonne, written on August 26, 1939, she is clearly trying to put on a brave face by extolling the need to regard the possibility of conflict within another, wider lens; and there is also perhaps a feeling of being bereft and in need of her friend: "I do feel that you and I are together in spirit and that this togetherness is indeed simply that we meet each other in Christ—and I am sure now that with us, His promise that when two or three are together in His name, He will be with them, is to be true—is true. . . . We will try, my dearest, you and I, to comfort one another's weakest moments and to encourage one another's best and bravest moments—and all will be well. Just like Juliana of Norwich says so often: All will be well—all is well."[27]

Later in the day, after a phone conversation with Yvonne, she repeats the need for Yvonne's courage and the sense of their togetherness. There is still the possibility that war may be averted, as everyone in the nation sits on the knife-edge. "Now I do feel we've just got to shut our eyes and dive into this sea of Christ, dive with the trust of people who can't swim and yet go straight into the dark water," she writes. And later in the letter: "I can't make my meaning clear, but I shall try to hang on to the thought all the time, that in a mysterious way everything that happens to us is not only His will, but Himself."[28]

Five days later, she writes that she is exhausted from the shambles that she has discovered at the First Aid Post ("our commandant, though very nice, seemed singularly devoid of both authority and method"), as well as the work she is stockpiling for both Father Bliss and *The Grail*, in case she does not survive what is coming ahead. She tries to put her thoughts together in a systematic form: "Never has my own heart so proved to me that the direct 'contemplation' of Christ in men, in the world, done not only through our minds, but through our bodies also, is the way to Him . . . and now I see, how without more than a necessary amount of egoism, we can even contemplate Him in our own life and come 'closer' to Him through it." She goes on: "The supreme comfort for me is, that the war which is threatened will not disturb our contemplation of Christ, but will complete it. . . . [I]t seems to me that one sound, or one pulse rather, fills the world, the beating of the heart of Christ, and so full of love it is, that one wishes only to put one's own heart into it to live and die in His passion with Him." Caryll finished the letter by telling Yvonne she had gone by the Grail's Sloane Street house, and wondering whether the windows were being blacked out in defense against air raids, she noted her own newly learned skill: "I've got pretty slick at 'black out' now!"[29]

On September 1, Hitler's forces invaded Poland. Two days later, Sunday, September 3, at 11:00 am, Caryll, Iris, and Joan sat before the radio and heard Prime Minister Chamberlain announce that Britain was now at war with Germany. The radio played "God Save the King," and immediately afterward an air raid siren pierced the air.

The next day Caryll wrote to Yvonne: "It is now forbidden to assemble big crowds of people together (owing to added danger in case of raids). . . . From the Grail point of view it seems to me good. It will force what *I*, at all events, have desired for a long time—i.e. the intensifying of real life in the world—and it will kill anything in the way of big-scale organizing. In other words, it has to be the kingdom *within* that counts!"[30] This was a point of information about obeying the wartime law, but more importantly for Caryll, it was also a declaration of her own negative opinion regarding the huge Grail rallies and the groupthink they spawned, an opinion that would resurface in the coming years.

Caryll, Iris, and Joan—soon to receive training on how to handle bomb casualties—were immediately put on regular first-aid duty. The First Aid Post was located at St. Mark's College in Chelsea, which proved to be rat-infested. Nothing seemed ready for them: ill-fitting gas masks, poorly fitting boots, and the lack of other equipment that seemed not to have reached them. Caryll set out her routine to Yvonne: "I am to work there three days a week in 12 hour shifts, i.e. Wednesday, Thursday, Friday, from 9:00 to 9:00 and then after two or three weeks it will be changed to three consecutive nights of 12 hour shifts." The physical effort alarmed her: "already my wretched lung is sore from being in gas proof rooms and gas masks."[31]

On September 6, she writes that she has a "cushy job" sitting by the telephone, a rare occurrence, she adds, because her allotted work is "nursing and gas," in spite of her lack of nursing ability. The relative leisure, while the phone remains silent, affords her the opportunity to express thoughts about the work she and Yvonne are engaged in together: "If we are ever to come back to the lovely morning of Christianity, we must not do it by waiting for the war to end; it has to be done now, through love. If each individual can put into her personal life an unstinted absolute love—then already out of these dark days Christ will be reborn." Then, apropos of what material to include in *The Grail*: "I feel strongly that so far as the 'written Word' is concerned, you should issue merely the simple statements of facts, how this war is Christ's passion—how Christ's passion redeems—how we are all 'other Christs' and so are now invited to enter His passion, and so on—just simple facts."[32]

As September wore on, with war having been declared but no war actually happening, life at the First Aid post began to take on an aspect of normality. "Everyone there is very nice," she wrote, "and it is lovely to see the realization of life without class distinctions and reduced to the simplest terms. I like the way we eat, only the plainest food, only what is necessary and from bare, scrubbed boards, no table cloths, no superfluous things of any sort (except rats!)"[33] It reminded her of a religious community, she wrote, and she even considered herself as a novice who had to do the lowly jobs of sweeping and scrubbing and submit in meek humility to admonitions when she did something incorrectly.

A week later, however, her physical energy had given way and she wrote: "I'd no idea I would hate it so heartily." The community around her at the First Aid Post had become "a kind of aching wound" that she approached "as to a lover's meeting just *because* it's like that. Often I have drawn the crucifix and now I know I shall draw it on myself." In an echo of her spiritual journal of a decade earlier, she accuses herself: "I'm miles away from entering His Passion as I would like to." She is not suffering enough, she writes; she indulges her whims when at home, reproving herself, and when people come to her "who so much need to be loved back into peace," she does not have the inner resources to help them. "I shall have to pray a lot before the little spark of my own life can truly be called Reparation."

Above all, in her state of total depletion she wants to be with Yvonne. During the night duty at the First Aid Post the workers must go to bed in a dormitory for three hours, and this experience is "like hell!" for her: "I hate the proximity of twenty other women!" And so she wraps herself in a "rug," or blanket, that she has brought from home and which she puts over her head, "and only then, when completely hidden in the rug and in the darkness, do I feel that I can let myself think openly about you. You're always in my mind, but all day I keep from dwelling on you; but in my rug, I think of you and I think how even death and the very Passion of Christ could be entered into more wholly, more joyously and far more gladly, if only I had more chance of delighting in loving you. I feel a real physical pang when I realize how little time we ever spent just being happy together." She goes on to write that "I now believe that love, human, personal love, is the root of all that is good, and that it is the greatest grace—just because the Religious System cripples and denies real love—I now feel perfectly sure that the Religious System is very bad indeed and so it is with many other old beliefs: they are gone."

How to unpack such a passage, written in a state of desperation and exhaustion? Is Caryll expressing an erotic longing, and is the Church, which she reveres and through which she is struggling to live the Christ-life, the "Religious System" she now seems to disdain? The question must remain largely unanswered, although it is possible that she is making a distinction, however confusing, between the church in its hierarchical-institution form and the church, which through the love of Christ becomes his mystical body. Immediately after, she writes: "So I lie in my rug and I think how happy I should be, could you but know that did I once feel your heart beating for me, I could rise on that strength and tenderness to the heart of Christ in His agony." Her love for Yvonne, then, is the means by which she enters Christ's Passion. Further in the letter she writes about Mary, the mother of Jesus. Mary and Yvonne then seem to be fused as she ends her rumination: "I myself in my rug, thinking of you, so desire this big strong element of a Mother!"[34]

The rug that gives her so much comfort does not prevent the

bed's fleas from jumping and keeping her awake. Caryll's life at this juncture—the discomfort and inconvenience of the First Aid Post along with her feeling of nursing incompetence, the longing for Yvonne's closeness, the uncertainty of everything—continues to feed her creative spirit. She wants Yvonne to give her some of Yvonne's own "great strength and courage to bear the love of God which seems to be more than so small a soul as mine can bear. How I wish, my lamb, that I need only write His name to you, or that together we could sit silent all day and keep the thought of Him in our hearts, without words at all. But no. I must remember that I am, besides the least of sinners, devil's advocate to the Grail." She then goes on with ideas and plans for *The Grail*. She tells Yvonne that she has begun to write a series of what she calls "Defences of the Mind." She wants them both—herself and Yvonne—to grasp the moment as Christ's Passion ("How, realizing the war as our share in the Passion, gives us a focus, a logical meaning, a way of gathering everything else into one whole, one sacrifice to offer through Christ") and to make connections in prayer with people of "any creeds who are capable in any degree for this work,"[35] with doctors and catechists, and with children who have been evacuated out of London.

Yvonne can hardly take it all in and is overwhelmed. Caryll assures her that she is still an infant "in the crook of its mother's arm," and Yvonne is the wise mother. She continues: "You ought not to fear my 'genius and overwhelming ideas' and I hope you won't for long. You know I am a very insufficient, frightened, helpless creature. I have no genius, only a little talent, and my only idea is to contemplate Christ in His life in people for so long as I live among people on earth and to do it with my whole being, hands, head, heart, etc.—not only with the mind."[36]

As the weeks went on, it became clear to Caryll that the First Aid Post was eating up her energy, with the regular twelve-hour days sometimes extended to eighteen hours, and days off sometimes canceled. Increased training was required "so as to become competent, as our best nurses will be sent to the front." But in spite of her exhaustion, the presence of Joan Wyndham, who was also stationed at the First Aid Post, brought youthful high spirits and good humor to the grim surroundings. As well, there was relief that she was wanted at the First Aid Post: "I felt relieved to be assured that they are not going to boot me out and if I can stick it myself, I can stay to bind up the wounds of this beloved city of mine."[37]

Apart from the First Aid Post and outpourings to Yvonne, care-free times still took place. Caryll, Iris, and Joan celebrated the last Christmas of the 1930s fulsomely with Midnight Mass, gifts, and a festive dinner. On Boxing Day, the circle of friends performed their Aladdin pantomime in the dining room of Milborne Grove and charged sixpence a ticket, with the proceeds going to the Loaves and Fishes. Men took women's parts, wearing Wendy's wigs and evening gowns, with arguments over which of them was to use the one roll of cotton wool in order to create a woman's bosom. Later in the day they had a tea party for the Sea-horses who had no one to spend Christmas with, and sang carols with them.

They toasted the new year of 1940 with the singing of "Auld Lang Syne," and a strong hot punch that left everyone tipsy. It was easy to forget at such a moment that Britain was at war, but stark reminders would come soon enough.

5

War
(1940–1944)

Now the time has come for each of us to prove our Christhood.
—This War Is the Passion

The first everyday sign that Britain was at war came in the form of food rationing in January 1940. Butter, sugar, and bacon were in short supply. Blackout regulations were still in force, and officially the country was on high alert, but the feeling of anxiety in London had lessened somewhat. People no longer stiffened and looked skyward at the sound of a plane, and most no longer carried their gas masks. The useless routine of the bandaging of healthy limbs continued at the First Aid Post, along with endless card-playing and other fill-in activities. Caryll spent her free time in the shed in the back garden of the Milborne Grove house, either writing or carving her latest sculpture, a pregnant Madonna in limewood. To her delight, to pass the time at the First Aid Post, carpentry lessons were taking place and she was allowed to carve when there was no pressing work to perform. Poetry and music were also encouraged as time-fillers.

And then, in lightning speed, there was war. In April, the Germans invaded Norway. In mid-May, news came that Holland,

Belgium, and France had fallen. Prime Minister Chamberlain resigned and was replaced by Winston Churchill. Air raid workers, having spent seven months playing cards and drinking tea, sprang into action. The nation rallied to help the British troops stranded in Dunkirk, and households double-checked their ability to obey the blackout rules.

By early summer, refugees were pouring into England from Belgium, and Caryll and Iris, glad to have someone to help, took on the task of entertaining Belgian children. In her work shed, Caryll taught them how to make toys. They decorated the toys and held an exhibition of them. Tea parties for the children were also held in the shed. The activities helped to calm the nerves, as uneasiness hung in the air. Caryll continued writing for Father Bliss's two publications, and, for *The Grail*, she pressed on with the ideas she had expounded in her letters to Yvonne: that the anxiety and fear hanging over the nation were a participation in the Passion of Christ. "This War Is the Passion" was the heading of one of her meditative pieces.

During the long summer evenings, Caryll's shed was the venue for poetry reading by Father Bliss, and friends would later recall occasions when he read aloud poems by Gerard Manley Hopkins. Father Corato was also a guest in the shed, arriving for liver-sausage suppers and drinking quantities of whiskey. There were gin parties with neighbors on Milborne Grove, and people spoke with faux bravery of a coming German invasion. The warm evening air filled the gatherings, a refuge from the heavy atmosphere of the First Aid Post. In mid-August there was news that the German air force was attacking British coastal defenses. Toward the end of the month the targets were aircraft factories and Royal Air Force bases. The sultry dusk was broken by the ominous sound of the air raid siren. On August 26, for the first time, Caryll and Iris hastened to the shelter that had been built in the back garden. The explosions, though far-off, were loud enough that the shelter shook and vibrated.

Then, on September 7, the nightly bombing of London, known as the Blitz, began. Casualties began pouring into the First Aid Post immediately. The blasts continued night after night, followed in the morning by the sight of rubble, dust, and debris. The numbers of people who were killed were tabulated daily. A week after the Blitz began, the journalist Mollie Panter-Downes, reporting for the magazine *The New Yorker*, wrote: "For Londoners, there are no longer such things as good nights; there are only bad nights, worse nights, and better nights." She went on to describe the sirens which went off the same time every evening and the queues of people outside the air-raid shelters holding babies and carrying blankets and thermos flasks. The raids, she wrote, were "directed against such military objectives as the tired shopgirl, the red-eyed clerk, and the thousands of dazed and weary families patiently trundling their few belongings in perambulators away from the wreckage of their homes."[1]

Caryll herself wrote: "We saw the illuminated 'S' that stands for shelter, and crawled down a spiral staircase that never seemed to end. We were in a disused underground railway station, hundreds of feet beneath the fires. It was a tunnel a mile long, and the walls were lined with rows of three-decker bunk beds. The track had been boarded up and now there were single bunks along the walls, then a gangway, then two rows pushed close together, another gangway, and another single row stretching on and on, until the eye could no longer follow them. . . . These shelters are fields, ploughed by the plough of God and waiting for seed."[2] The bombing—first the paralyzing fear, then the violent crashes—terrified Iris. Caryll, terror-stricken herself, took to making up silly games, pretending she was a puppet on a string, in an effort to distract her friend.

On October 20, nearly two months after the Blitz began and a month after Caryll's thirty-ninth birthday, a series of bombs landed in the vicinity of Milborne Grove, one of them three houses away from Iris and Caryll's home. Their house suffered damage to its foundation: windows blown in, the doors jammed. The neighborhood lay in near ruins. Iris was the first to discover the damage, and she left immediately to find accommodation elsewhere. She found the only flat available in the apartment block known as the Nell

Gwynn House on Sloane Street. It was a one-room unfurnished flat with minimal kitchen facilities and a bathroom. This was to be home for herself, Joan, and Caryll. The three dragged mattresses from Milborne Grove through the streets, and with their bicycles they carried other necessary items to their new abode. The only piece of furniture that they could fit in the flat was a table that Iris bought from the hall porter for five shillings.

Their new home address meant that new habits had to be formed. For daily Mass, they began going to the Brompton Oratory or the centuries-old St. Mary's Church on Cadogan Street, picking their way through the debris and the smell of burnt rubble. Their housemaid, Kate, continued to work for them, shopping for food and doing their laundry. And like millions of other misplaced Londoners, they continued on with their work regardless of their new circumstances, facing their shattering fear and the violence around them as best they could. The shed at the back of the Milborne Grove house had not been affected by the bomb, and so Caryll continued to work there, writing for Father Bliss and *The Grail*, carving a set of Stations of the Cross, and producing a set of illustrations for a book called *New Six O'Clock Saints*, later to be published by Sheed & Ward.[3] As the war went on, there would be a shortage of wood for carving, as well as pens and pencils for writing.

Two months after their forced move, Caryll was nearly killed in a raid as she was rushing home along Sloane Street. "I saw the thing coming; it was a land mine and they shot it in the air," she wrote to her friend, Henry Tayler, and then, "suddenly the whole sky went a dull cruel crimson. I thought, 'I'd better get down on the ground.'"[4] Sometime later, still flat on the ground, she thought she could hear the ringing of bells, and then next thing she knew rescue workers were helping her up and she saw that she was surrounded by the shattered glass from shop windows.

In the meantime, Caryll's writing in *The Grail* was being read by a woman in the United States who would soon be instrumental in changing her life. The woman's name was Maisie Ward. She was fifty-one years of age and, with her husband, Frank Sheed, was one-half of the publisher Sheed & Ward. Maisie was a prominent member of the English Catholic intellectual tradition and had a family connection to the aristocracy. Later described by her son as "part Major Barbara, part scholastic theologian,"[5] she was the somewhat reserved daughter of the English Catholic biographer Wilfred Ward and his wife, the novelist Josephine Hope. On her mother's side she was related to the Duke of Norfolk, the premier Catholic aristocrat in England. The Oxford Movement and John Henry Newman had been influential in conversions on both sides of her family, and by the time Maisie was born, Catholicism permeated the family's day-to-day life. She had married Frank Sheed, eight years her junior, an ebullient and quick-witted Australian, who, although baptized in his mother's Catholic faith, had been brought up a Protestant at his father's insistence. Teenage rebellion against his alcoholic father had returned him back to Catholicism by the time he landed in London.

Frank and Maisie met within the earnest milieu of the Catholic Evidence Guild, which sought to explain the Catholic faith within an everyday setting, mainly through talks, and for which Maisie wrote the speakers' training manual. She herself was already a seasoned lecturer. Frank quickly learned how to expound on Catholic theology at Speaker's Corner, on the corner of Hyde Park and the Marble Arch, his loud voice and enthusiastic speech—sounding "like a revolutionary calling one to the barricades"[6]—often attracting modest crowds. In 1925, Frank and Maisie's brother Leo formed a publishing company called Sheed & Ward to make available to the British public the writing of Catholic intellectual thinking that had recently come of age (when Leo left to study for the priesthood, Maisie became the Ward half of the company). By 1940, they were publishing the leading English Catholic writers of the day, including G. K. Chesterton, Hilaire Belloc, and Ronald Knox, as well as English translations of work by leaders of the French Catholic Renaissance such as Jacques Maritain and Etienne Gilson. The couple also became writers in their own right. Maisie published the two-volume study of her own family, *The Wilfred*

Wards, and Frank wrote short, easy-to-understand works on Catholic doctrine such as *A Map of Life*. By the mid-thirties they became successful enough as a publishing company that they decided to open an American office in New York. For the duration of the war years, Frank often crossed the Atlantic on a special permit to keep an eye on the London office while Maisie remained at their home with their two children in Pennsylvania.

Both were enthusiastic about Caryll's writing in *The Grail*. From the United States, Maisie wrote to the editor of the publication, who was still Yvonne, to ask about the possibility of publishing some of the material in book form. Before the year was over, Frank and Yvonne were meeting with Caryll in London to discuss the proper order of the articles as well as additional material needed for the book.

Caryll had the shed in the back of the Milborne Grove house as a place to write. For the first time in her writing life, however, she seems to have been temporarily seized with writers' block: it was one thing to write out her thoughts about the Passion of Christ in a stumbling fashion to Yvonne and then to include them in an anonymous article; it was another to work them into a book so as to satisfy an editor across the Atlantic Ocean. In December, she wrote to Henry Tayler: "I don't get on with my book. . . . When I get the pen in hand to start, I am paralysed; I feel a real skunk, not at all fit to write about Christ in others."[7]

As the year drew to a close, fatigue as a result of sleepless nights and disrupted lives was taking its toll throughout London. Thousands of people had been killed in the bombings, and even more thousands had been wounded. People were wearily used to the air raid sirens and the eerie quiet after the bombardments and then emerging from shelters to find only crumbling walls where buildings used to be. The frigid winter weather became another burden, and Caryll later wrote: "It's true I've just been at the limit of my endurance. I think the cold makes everything more tiring and having to come to anchor after work and then go out and face another cold journey defeats me."[8]

For Christmas Eve and the night of Christmas Day in 1940, however, no bombs were dropped over London. Two days later, Caryll wrote that "however mixed and tangled the motives," the twenty-four-hour respite from violence "was so wonderful; it gave one hope for the world: man after all has great good in him and there *can* be peace on earth." Pope Pius XII had given permission to have midnight Mass earlier in the evening because of the night raids. For Caryll, with London *in extremis*, the Christmas Eve Mass was especially beautiful: "[T]he church was filled, literally filled, with burning candles and scarlet camellias." The scene "was so glowing and so in contrast to the greyness, the ruins, the cynicism, the tears, outside that it made one feel as if one was literally *inside* the heart of Christ." On Christmas Day, the exhausted workers at the First Aid Post were treated to a feast of "turkey, plum pudding, trifle, chocolates, lemonade and crackers."[9]

Caryll (right) and Iris, lounging at home in the late 1930s. Courtesy Camilla Shivarg.

Five nights after the Christmas pause came the bombing raid that would become known as the "second great fire of London."[10] The attack came in the area of warehouses and offices, including most of the offices of London's publishers, around St. Paul's Cathedral. Joan Wyndham described the night's raid as "the full blast of the Nazi fury," and recorded her experience of it in her diary/ memoir: "The aeroplanes never stopped and the sound of their engines dive-bombing was deafening. . . . The sky was already red as blood—it looked as if half London was on fire. Flares lit up the street like daylight and the stars were all put out."[11]

Among the casualties of the fire was the London office of Sheed & Ward. From the safety of the United States, Maisie received the shocking news from her husband: "I left the office and went down to Oxford. On Monday morning I came back bright and early to the office and there wasn't any office—just a handful of bricks in a hole. The big incendiary raid of the night before had wiped out most of Paternoster Row. Of our place nothing at all survived—all our books were destroyed and all our records. . . . The only member of the staff to show any sign of emotion was one of our packers, who gave one look and then brought up his breakfast."[12] In an earlier letter, Frank had described the resilient spirit that had quickly become a hallmark of Londoners who were suffering the nightly barrage of bombs: "The mood is not of anger, but only of complete determination. Their attitude to the Germans is rather like one's attitude to the plague. One does not get angry at microbes; but only determined to stop them."[13]

Despite this major publishing setback, as if their establishment needed only a mere dusting off, Frank wrote: "We are taking another office nearby and hope to be running more or less normally again in a month or two."[14] Caryll's book, called *This War Is the Passion*, was published in the United States by Sheed & Ward a few weeks later. The title was taken from the first meditation in the book: the exact words had been expressed in one of Caryll's letters to Yvonne. The book's thesis was laid out on the first page: "Because he has made us 'other Christs', because his life continues in each one of us, there is nothing that any one of us can suffer which is not the passion he suffered."[15]

The United States was soon to enter the war, and the book was an immediate success. (Later, when the first royalty check arrived, Caryll's first payment of any substance, she handed it to Iris.) The text anticipated Pope Pius XII's encyclical on the mystical body of Christ, which would be issued two years later, and it was a tangible expression of Father Steuart's more theological and abstract writing on the mystical body. Much of its power came from the concreteness of Caryll's own life: the stress and fear, the dislocation, the grime and bomb wreckage, the lives lost, the daily uncertainty about what lay ahead.

The young Jesuit, Bernard Lonergan (himself displaced by the war, having been sent from Rome back to his native Canada just days before he was to defend his doctoral dissertation), wrote: "Faith is dynamite, and every so often it explodes. This is what happened in the series of essays that form *This War Is the Passion*." Under the mistaken impression that Caryll was a member of the Grail,[16] he wrote of the movement's "mystical faith" and went on to liken the book's author to such spiritual geniuses as Augustine and Benedict, whose creative work broke through the barbarism of their day. In Caryll Houselander's case, he wrote, with "flashes of spiritual insight" she breaks through the "dry rot" of Western culture by highlighting "faith in the Mystical Body of Christ in whom we are all one, from whom we draw the bread and bloodstream of life, to whom we return in the consummation of charity that thinks no evil and refuses no good." He echoed Caryll herself: "[W]e have our bodies and our souls to give to God, and that was all Christ had, that was all the Apostles had."[17]

The simplicity of the book's language and the use of everyday words made its contents accessible to everyone, along with the comforting assurance that the author was sharing her readers' wartime experience of worry, grief, and anguish as they cleared the rubble of their lives. Her cat, Jones, made his way into the meditations: "My cat—I can't neglect him for long, as to-day he is my spiritual director!—is a tabby," she writes and then remarks on how the cat, seized with fear at the menacing approach of a giant tomcat, then purred with contentment once he was settled on her lap: a lesson in learning "to receive the love of God."[18] She was later delighted to learn that the cat's presence in the book's pages was the favorite part of the book for many people, especially among soldiers. She was astounded by the letters she received from readers of the book who told her that her words about suffering applied not only to their war experiences, but perhaps more deeply to other aspects of their lives as well. Among Caryll's annoyances, however, as she gradually became well known, was Cardinal Bernard Griffin's insistence on referring to her, now in her fortieth year, as "a young English girl."

Caryll and her cat, Jones, in front of her bomb-damaged home, late 1940. Courtesy Camilla Shivarg.

Even in Britain, where the book had not yet been published, many people seem to have gotten hold of it, and as a result, Caryll received letter after letter asking for her advice. She answered every one and was now busier than ever with this extra load as well as work for Father Bliss, in addition to the ongoing work at the First Aid Post, which left her limp with exhaustion. A new involvement also came her way: this was a request from Dr. Eric Strauss, a prominent psychiatrist at St. Bartholomew's Hospital, to work with some of his young patients.

It is not known how Dr. Strauss came to be aware of Caryll, but it may have been through his friendship with the Farm Street Jesuits. (One of the Jesuits, Philip Caraman, had recommended Dr. Strauss to the novelists Evelyn Waugh and Graham Greene.) Dr. Strauss's background and interests were varied and rich: as a young man he had served in World War I and then had studied neurology, subsequently moving into the field of psychiatry. He also composed music and was an accomplished pianist. At some point he converted to Catholicism, likely at the Farm Street Church, and developed an interest in Thomistic theology. His approach to psychiatry was holistic, and he believed that the arts could play a role in helping some of his afflicted patients. Personally, he was a courteous and highly cultured man, and it may have been a shock when he met Caryll face-to-face, to discover a woman who had not only a clownish appearance, but also the mouth of a street brawler. He asked her not to use vulgar language with the children because some of them were very sensitive: "I am apt to slip upon this language and find myself on the edge of vulgar slang now and then, but so far have remembered in time!" she wrote to Henry Tayler.[19]

The children whom Caryll worked with had probably been badly affected mentally by the bombing, and what she did with them, having sometimes only one, and at other times as many as four or five, was a form of art therapy. She was able to meet with them at her work shed in the back garden of the Milborne Grove house. As a musician himself, Dr. Strauss thought that music would be a particular help, and for this she enlisted the assistance of Henry, who was a pianist. Henry, about ten years younger than Caryll, was a convert to Catholicism, likely through friendship with her. They had been friends since the early thirties, and he had become part of her close circle. Henry had gotten a job as an accountant at the Catholic Truth Society, and would eventually become the executor of Caryll's will.

"Dr. Strauss has written to me in a very encouraging way about the work I'm doing for Pedro," she wrote to Henry in 1942. "I find that working for him I am able to put into practice all my theories about psychology and I have great hope that from our poor little shed and this one strange, lovely boy, our wisdom school may really begin."[20] Her letters to Henry, as the war wore on, referred to a religious book store combined with a "wisdom school" that the two would develop, along with a new friend, Archie Campbell-Murdoch, who was a teacher, once the nation was at peace. The plans—possibly war-time pipe dreams—came to nothing.

Caryll's letters to Henry during the early years of the 1940s suggest that he had replaced Yvonne as the person upon whom she poured her passionate affection. Whereas Yvonne had been the mother figure, Henry became the lover or "boyfriend" figure. In one letter she likens him to a divinity: she describes a visit to Woolworth's, the department store where in "a mere jolly and vulgar day dream" she wanted to buy him something, as if "I was walking and talking with you, much as Adam did with God, and really I daresay Woolworth's is the nearest we can get to Eden in the modern world and I'm sure the man one loves is the nearest we can get in human creature to God!"[21] Henry is "Dearest" and "Darling" in the letters, and in 1942, when he was deputized to leave London and join the Home Guard, she wrote that her "chief happiness" in her newly published book "is that it comes just at this time when we are parted more, and it can take my place talking to you. It's not a good book, but I'd gladly write a thousand books and be ashamed of them if they would be me in your pocket!"[22] And, in a later letter, telling him that an aunt of hers has gotten married at a relatively advanced age, she adds: "Well, my sweet, it ought to encourage us, not to be too shy to marry when we are 70!!"[23]

There is an indication that Henry, like Yvonne, is overwhelmed by Caryll's passionate intensity toward him; and so she responds: "You say you can't integrate the mush I talk. . . . But so far as there is anything worth integrating in my spate of talk: has it not occurred to you that it is so very *very* often *you* who have given it to me, and it is just because *you have given it* that you can't take it into yourself in the way you want to?"[24] In fact, it is likely that, like Yvonne, there was something in Henry's personality—perhaps a personal sensitivity and an artistic sensibility—that drew Caryll to work out her thoughts in letters to him.

Early on, Caryll had applied for work in the Censorship Office, and in 1942 she began to work there, censoring letters first and then parcels, up to a hundred a day. A year earlier, she had written to Henry about her attitude to her war work: "[I]t seems to bring before my eyes all the wounds and anxieties and courage and pathetic joys of the people of the world. I am able to pray for each one, to offer sacrifices when that seems to be called for, to commend them all to God. . . . It never occurred to me that this sort of continual prayer for people would arise out of this job; now I wonder it did not, for it is inevitable."[25]

A co-worker in the Censorship Office, Christine Spender, sister of the poet Stephen Spender, remembered in later years that Caryll's dignity of bearing overcame her odd appearance. When they first became acquainted, Caryll prayed to know whether she was meant to "take me on," which Christine understood to mean the question of whether she was to become one of Caryll's friends. If the oddness of this approach put off some co-workers, the peculiarity of it was offset by Caryll's witty banter. Likewise, when Christine's cat died on, as it happened, the feast of the Virgin Mary's birth, Caryll said in response to Christine's sadness, "Perhaps Our Lady has taken your little white cat for her birthday present!"[26] Rather than remarking on the sticky sweet sentimentality of the response, Christine accepted it in the spirit of simplicity and found it oddly comforting.

Caryll presented a more steely side of herself in a letter to Archie Campbell-Murdoch. Regarding the hordes of needy people seeking her help and made even more desperate by the war, Caryll wrote: "Actually, even if one can escape in body, one's mind remains guilt-obsessed, accusing and restless, haunted by tottering old ladies, subversive and over-sensitive youths, frustrated geniuses, spineless adolescents, dying priests, doubting Anglican clergymen, repressed

Catholic nuns, neurasthenic nurses, and the uncountable multitude of weeping free-lance virgins."[27]

In 1943, Iris joined Caryll at the Censorship. The work itself demanded less physical energy, but it still met with constant exhaustion and meals snatched on the run. When the female workers were hired for work in Censorship they were issued a large sheet of brown paper which was to be used when the air raid siren sounded; they were to place it on the floor under the table and crouch upon it, thus saving their skirts from the dust of the floor.

Working at the Censorship meant that Caryll had a more regular weekly routine. Her day began with 7 o'clock Mass and was followed by her Censorship work, which took place during regular business hours. In the day-and-a-half she had off each week she managed to fit in her work with the child patients of Dr. Strauss, as well as the work she now considered central: her book manuscripts. In addition, she was doing nearly all the writing for the *Children's Messenger* out of loyalty to Father Bliss. And now there was, in addition, the "stream of callers" who had discovered her through her book: "They are usually aged ladies without homes, friends, etc., utterly lonely, *really* lonely soldiers who are misfits in their local units, or children who wish to confide." Plus, she added, "continual running repairs to myself, washing up, cleaning the room, feeding the cat, sewing on buttons and patching and darning the rags I once called 'my clothes.'"[28]

Caryll also volunteered her time as a nighttime fire warden on the roof of the Nell Gwynn House, looking out over the miles of darkness, and in a letter written after the war she explained how this decision came about. During the air raids, she wrote, she tried not to be frightened, but to muster her courage with the help of prayer. "Then one day I realized quite suddenly, as long as I try not to be afraid I shall be worse, and I shall show it one day and break; what God is asking of me, to do for suffering humanity, is to *be* afraid, to accept it and put up with it." This insight did not lessen her fear, she said, "I've often had to resort to sheer force to hide the fact that my teeth were chattering." But, she added, "I felt that God had put His hand right down through all the well upon well of darkness and horror between Him and me and was holding the central point of my soul; and I knew that *however afraid I was then, it would not, even could not, break me.*" After this, she said that on the roof of Nell Gwynn House, surrounded by the dark city, she "always knew God was there in a special way, to accept the offering of fear."[29]

By spring 1943, there were still air raids, some killing dozens of people, but they had ceased to be a nightly occurrence over London. Winston Churchill had given his cautionary "end of the beginning" speech the previous November,[30] but a touch of normality began to return. The nerve-wracking anxiety that attended daily life still existed to some extent, as did constant line-ups for shopping and the scarcity of goods. But there were also casual walks in the park. In the back garden of Milborne Grove, blossoming trees surrounded Caryll's shed, where she continued to work. She once again entertained friends to suppers of liver sausage or spam omelette. A year earlier, she had managed to secure her own flat in Nell Gwynn House. The flat was small, with little light, and was located on the ground floor at the back of the building. In a touch of dark humor Caryll called it the "Kitch Morgue." But it provided solitude and privacy and allowed her to have poetry readings with Father Bliss, once again, as well as musical evenings with Henry, with whom she listened to Bach on the gramophone. The ground-floor flat also accorded her the possibility of climbing out the window to escape if knocks on her door became incessant.

The parties of yore were infrequent, if held at all: although liquor was not rationed, shopkeepers sold only a bottle or so a month to regular customers. Gin, favored by Caryll, was manufactured from imported spirits and thus in short supply. She told Archie Campbell-Murdoch that she now avoided parties. The consequences of living under direct bomb attack during wartime along with her newfound fame had brought changes in Caryll: "I am so conscious of being grotesque, ill-dressed, awkward and talking too much that it is a torture to me to go anywhere and this is always followed by several days of remorse," she wrote.[31]

She had become encouraged by the praise that Frank Sheed had given her work, and fortified with that encouragement she had begun to write what she called an "Our Lady" book. In July she gave Frank her typescript for the book, which she titled "The Bride and the Spirit." Frank wrote to his wife: "The Houselander Our Lady seems to me an absolute honey. Exactly the level of *This War Is the Passion*: there's a splash of genius in that funny little thing."[32]

Frank's encouragement at that time was important to her, because for more than a year she had been embroiled in a complaint lodged by her close friend, Yvonne Bosch van Drakestein. Yvonne claimed that as editor of *The Grail*, she had the right to some of the copyright of *This War Is the Passion*. As well, she argued, the ideas expressed in the book were hers, and Caryll had, like a scribe, put Yvonne's ideas into words. Thus she and *The Grail* should have a share in the royalties from the book. On April 30, 1942, Caryll wrote to Henry: "I've been very sad over Yvonne who revealed in a burst of bad humour or nerves that they consider themselves wronged and aggrieved because Sheed & Ward have not attributed my book to them in some way. They now want to make out that I am somehow beholden to them for writing at all! I can't really grasp just what they want, but I do grasp that they think me unfair, ungrateful and ungenerous! However, don't repeat any of that."[33]

The problem dragged on for several months. On December 28, she wrote to Henry again: "Dearest, please pray hard for me. A simply dreadful situation has arisen over Yvonne. I felt nearly too ill to move on Xmas day as the result of it."[34] And to Archie, she wrote of "some very bitter trouble over Xmas." She went on to say that "it was as heavy on me as anything could be, and I felt almost as near despairing as I could do. I do not mean despairing of God's mercy, but of my work ever doing anything but go awry and give pain."[35]

In the end, an agreement was reached between Sheed & Ward and Yvonne, and permission was given to *The Grail* to publish its own imprint of *This War Is the Passion*. As a result, in 1943, under the title *Defences of the Mind*, the essays were published as they had originally appeared in *The Grail*, with Caryll named as the author and the Grail as the publisher. At the same time, *This War Is the Passion* was finally published in Britain under Sheed & Ward's imprint. At the bottom of the copyright page was written: "All the Articles in this book were written for the Grail Magazine and are now reprinted with the Editor's permission."

At the beginning of 1944, Caryll wrote what she described to Henry as "what I must consider as the letter confirming my final break with Yvonne."[36] She later wrote that she had never agreed with the Grail's group-mindedness and what she perceived as a tendency toward catering to "respectable Catholics." Her writing was done out of love for Yvonne alone, she explained, rather than for the Grail itself. She also felt slighted by the members of the movement, not having ever been invited to join the Grail, and she may have perceived an attitude of snobbishness as she regarded the mental picture of herself, scrawny and shabby, weighed down with work and exhaustion, beside the stylishly dressed Grail members who bloomed with health and vitality. "I have never been helped by them spiritually; even when I asked Yvonne for help and advice in the beginning, I never got it: verbal requests met with silence, letters were ignored. I have never been allowed into a Grail Retreat either," she wrote to Henry.[37]

This was as far as Caryll would go in direct critique of Yvonne personally, and though their friendship cooled considerably, neither of them spoke ill of the other. Yvonne would insist in the future that her conflict had been with Sheed & Ward and not with Caryll. Caryll herself would continue to take umbrage at *The Grail*'s continued use of copyrighted material, including the drawings of a new friend, Diana Orpen (known as "Dickie"), the daughter of the portrait painter Sir William Orpen and an artist in her own right, whom Caryll had met through her First Aid work: "I can't tell you how appalled I am over that fearful cribbing of Dickie Orpen's drawings," she wrote to Frank Sheed. "It makes me really furious when I consider that the cribber is exempt from war service on the grounds (I suppose) of being full time 'Youth Leader' and has her whole time free to copy other people's work, while Dickie, the real *owner* of the work, has literally flogged them out of an exhausted will after a full day or night of nursing." By this time, Yvonne had passed on the editorial duties of *The Grail* to someone whom Caryll described as "a healthy young woman in her twenties who is exempted to have time to encourage others to die nicely!"[38]

In the meantime, Caryll's "Our Lady" book was all set to come into the world. It was given a new title, *The Reed of God*, and published in 1944. The book is a spiritual study of Mary, the mother of Jesus, that takes the reader along meandering thoughts through the life of Jesus. Each section consists of short paragraphs, almost extended aphorisms that lead the reader into Caryll's thoughts about Mary. The characteristics of Caryll's earlier book remained: simple sentences using concrete images relating to people's everyday lives, juxtaposed with startling spiritual insights. The book's title image, the reed, like a wind instrument of music, is a hollowed-out, empty space, and this, Caryll writes, is what Mary provided: a space for Christ to grow in her. She uses two other container images as well: a cup and a bird's nest, and it was likely Frank Sheed, as editor, who highlighted the reed as the central image by putting it in the book's title.

The central motif of the book is Mary as Christ-bearer and, thus, the model for all Christians. "The one thing she did and does is the one thing that we all have to do, namely, to bear Christ into the world,"[39] she writes, and goes on to enumerate in detail what she means: "All the time spent in earning a living, cleaning the home, caring for the children, making and mending clothes, cooking," and then "it is really through ordinary human life and the things of every hour of every day that union with God comes about."[40]

The book follows the events of Mary's life—the Annunciation, Advent ("the season of the seed"),[41] the birth and childhood of Jesus, the loss of Jesus in the temple, the Crucifixion, the Assumption. "Washing, weaving, kneading, sweeping, her hands prepared

His hands for the nails," she writes, her words, like poetry, pointing to something profound beyond themselves. She connects birth and death, always circling back to the Passion of Christ—"The swaddling bands were the first burial bands."[42]

She alludes several times to the war in the book, and it is clear that her awareness is in the here and now: crumbling ruins all around her in London, refugees who are now beginning to pour in from the continent.[43] The book made Caryll Sheed & Ward's star author. "Sales go on in pleasant volume," Frank wrote to Maisie, "but no one book has the bit in its teeth yet except *Reed of God*, which sold 367 last week and has already reached 167 this week."[44]

By early 1944, there was already talk that the Allied forces were planning an invasion of occupied Europe, and as talk intensified, a new phenomenon of war appeared over London: flying-bombs, also known as doodlebugs. A notice now greeted everyone at the entrance to the Censorship that read, in large black letters: IMMI-NENT DANGER. There was a new tension in the air as workers stiffened and held their breath while flying bombs whirred and buzzed overhead. They relaxed only when the bombs passed and landed somewhere farther along. Once again, sirens wailed nearly every night. Exhausted Londoners, who hoped that the war was nearly over, piled again into air raid shelters.

In April 1944, Caryll received the surprise of a letter from Maisie Ward, who had written to congratulate her on the publication of *The Reed of God*. Up to now, Caryll's connection to Sheed & Ward had been through the friendly and outgoing Frank Sheed, whom she regarded as savior and advocate and with whom she had established an easy friendship. It is not known how much Caryll knew about Maisie's aristocratic connections or her important place in the English Catholic intellectual revival, but her reply reflects a sense of awe. She addresses Maisie as "Mrs. Sheed," and her writing is, at the beginning at least, deferential. She is amazed that Frank has praised her writing: "I quite honestly feel very acutely aware of how amateurish and queer my writing is," and as if to emphasize her own state of lowliness: "I certainly will try not to fail you and I shall always do my best, but I am always aware of a kind of disintegration in myself, a crumbling and falling apart, and being only kept together at all by a miracle, *the* miracle of the creative Love of God."[45]

A few weeks later, her new correspondent in the United States became "My dear Maisie," and it was clear an intimacy had developed between them in a very short time. It is possible that Caryll, with her winsomeness, candor, and intensity of language in which she spoke of God as readily as her own daily life, struck a sympathetic chord within Maisie who was struggling with her own spiritual life. By now, Maisie had raised an idea to Caryll: that they produce a book on the rosary. The book would contain paintings of the medieval Italian artist Fra Angelico depicting the decades of the rosary. Maisie would write the explanatory text, and Caryll would write a prayer for each decade.

Caryll was in ready agreement, but already looking ahead to postwar conditions: "[S]omething that is knocking at our hearts all day long, a question: namely, are the lives that we are going to live after this war going to be an answer to those who have suffered and died that we may live at all, or are we going to sink back to what we were before and betray all those who have died and all those who have lived lives that were living deaths in Europe—and above all, the supreme question for me is, am I going to witness the Passion with my own eyes and not be changed at all by it?"[46]

In a later letter, Caryll told Maisie that she wrote the prayers for the rosary book during the worst of the flying bomb attacks while taking cover in shelters, during which "something which has been growing on me all through the war came to a crescendo: namely an intensely clear awareness of the utter insignificance of war compared to the Eternal things."[47] That same spring of 1944, Caryll received an invitation from the Anglican Bishop of Southampton to give a talk at a meeting of clergy to be held at Oxford in July; the Anglican response to *This War Is the Passion* had been highly positive. Maisie suggested something similar: that Caryll should consider a lecture trip to the United States. Caryll declined: "I am not and never could be a lecturer, I haven't the gifts or the nerve or even the voice for it, I have not a spot of charm or personality and my voice is toneless."[48]

On the occasion of the Anglican invitation, however, she accepted. She made meticulous notes and plans in preparation for her talks. Iris accompanied Caryll to Oxford, and they stayed in the Randolph Hotel, their first experience of grandeur for many years. Both were seized with nervousness, Caryll because she had no experience in public speaking and was unsure of how she would be received among Church of England clergy, and Iris because her naturally nervous temperament had intensified during the war years. The talk took place at Wadham College, and the audience consisted of two bishops, forty other clergymen, and one woman, who Caryll thought was probably the wife of one of the clergy members. Iris paced the street as Caryll spoke inside. Caryll later reported that after a burst of stage fright, she spoke naturally. She found her audience to be warm and sincere listeners who laughed loudly at her humor.

"What fun about Caryll and the 40 parsons: she might take Evelyn Underhill's place and what a job she would do,"[49] Frank wrote to Maisie, referring to the Anglican spiritual writer who had become the first woman to address a gathering of clergy and who had died shortly after the beginning of the war. Although Caryll said in letters that she spoke to various groups of people, there is no record that she spoke again publicly. She did, however, receive invitations to contribute to various publications. And in a letter to Archie she wrote: "A nun in America has written to say she wants to write an article on me and asks for 'intimate details' of my life!! Good Heavens! There are *no* intimate details at all suitable for it! And I tremble knowing what American publicity can do." The same letter reveals Caryll as overwhelmed with work, none of which has anything to do with her day job, which is still at the Censorship: "I have been going too slowly and falling asleep at night, at my table, as if I had been poleaxed, consequently things are overdue." She enumerated the work she had committed herself to: material for the *Messenger* as well as *The Children's Messenger*, a design for a tombstone for someone in India, pamphlets, articles, illustrations for children's books, "plus innumerable letters that must somehow be answered."[50] In addition, she had also agreed to read manuscripts that had been submitted to Sheed & Ward.

In her letters to Maisie, Caryll continued to cast herself as a trifling writer in comparison with Maisie's greatness. When it came to some other matters, however, she wrote almost as Maisie's spiritual director. By the end of summer 1944, she was pouring her thoughts into letters of multiple pages, much as she had with Yvonne, and to a lesser extent, with Henry. By now, her thoughts had turned to psychological matters—the sense of guilt, in particular. She had been reading about psychology for many years and was developing her own theories. She told Maisie about the experience of her childhood illness, and on reflection she decided that the root of the illness was guilt. (There may also have been a sense of guilt stemming from her parents' separation.)

For her part, Maisie was writing to Caryll about her own struggles with guilt. Among Maisie's worries was the condition of her teenaged son, Wilfred, who had been stricken with polio. Another struggle had to do with her friendship with the American Catholic activist Dorothy Day, whom she admired immensely and compared with whom she considered herself to have a "limping life"[51] that she was ashamed of. A particular point on which she could not agree with Dorothy Day's position, however, was the question of pacifism in the face of war.

This was a sore point with Maisie, who believed that Britain had been justified in declaring war against Germany. Caryll's lengthy response suggests that Maisie was torn up over her disagreements with her activist friend. She sided with Maisie and came to the conclusion that Dorothy Day's Christianity was too narrowly focused: "I believe that even the greatest saint is incomplete, considered alone, that each individual attains his Christhood only by being part of the whole Body of Christ, and only through the giving and taking of one to another, and that the more intensely and completely that an individual is himself, the more completely is he the part of a whole—the Whole Christ."[52] And in a letter a few weeks later she departs from Dorothy Day while still admiring her: "If only DD could realize it, pacifism is a terrible separator. Personally I hate war, I am ready to swear more than she does too and with more reason—but I would never be a pacifist because in taking part in a war, one takes one's share of the common burden."[53]

By September 1944, the war's end was in sight. People were greeting each other with the assurance that the fighting would soon be over. Caryll was physically exhausted from anemia and lack of sleep, but made no mention of her health in letters to Maisie. "We are rejoicing in the idea of no more Flying Bombs and distinctly less black out!"[54] Caryll wrote in September. A sign of the easing of restrictions: a trip to the theater to see the play *Arsenic and Old Lace*. And as 1944 drew to a close, the beginning of postwar plans.

6

Postwar
(1945–1949)

What a motley crowd they were, these saints of our times!
—The Dry Wood

By the beginning of 1945, Londoners were increasingly making postwar plans. Iris Wyndham's anxiety throughout the noise and destruction of London's bombardments had never abated, but she kept a sign of hope on her blotting paper at the Censorship. This was a postcard that featured the pastoral scene of a quaint woodland cottage. Now, with the assurance of Allied victory soon to be declared, she bought a cottage deep in the countryside. The cottage sat in a field outside the village of Terrick, near Aylesbury, in Buckinghamshire. Cottage living was still in the future, however, and for the time being the small structure remained empty.

Caryll's books had become well known among English Catholics. More than once in confession she was advised by a confessor to read either *This War Is the Passion* or *The Reed of God*. In early 1945, she wrote to Archie Campbell-Murdoch: "Oh, here is a bit of egotistical news, which will amuse you. I have had a 'fan' letter from Monsignor Ronald Knox, about *The Reed of God*."[1] Monsignor Knox, at the age of fifty-seven, was one of the best known and most highly acclaimed Catholic writers of the day. He famously converted to Catholicism as a brilliant young Anglican priest three decades earlier, and in addition to his religious writings, was also the author of a series of mystery novels. By this time he had embarked on an English translation of the whole Bible. Knox was the friend of Catholic aristocrats as well as acclaimed Catholic writers such as Evelyn Waugh. But in his letter to Caryll he exposed something more personal about himself, perhaps, than he did with his better-known friends. He referred to the book's section on Jesus as the lost child, and in particular one sentence spoke to him of his own spiritual state: "The lyrical young Christ that was the youth of our soul has gone away, leaving us a dyspeptic old man, lonely in a cluttered room of his own making, a forgotten invalid sitting in a timeless twilight of mediocrity."[2] Had he found a kindred soul in the writer of the simple text? Caryll wrote to Archie that Monsignor Knox's letter was "not a 'fan' in the vulgar sense; it's an incredibly humble and moving little note."[3]

In early May 1945, the air raid sirens stopped, a signal that a formal announcement would soon be made regarding Allied victory. Rationing did not yet come to an end (nor would it for a number of years), but luxury items such as ice cream began to appear in shops. And finally: it was V-E Day, May 8. The German army had surrendered the day before, and an announcement was made that V-E Day would be a holiday for everyone. Caryll began the big day with High Mass at Westminster Cathedral, after which the congregation sang "God Save the King." The writer Molly Panter-Downes noted that during the day there were "no salutes of guns, only the pealing of the bells and the whistles of tugs on the Thames . . . and the roar of the planes, which swooped back and forth over the city."[4] Joan Wyndham, who had joined the Women's Auxiliary Air Force in Lancashire four years earlier at the age of twenty, arrived back in London on a morning train and found Iris and Caryll already celebrating with a bottle of sherry. Caryll's teddy bear, Roosy, sat in a place of honor with a Union Jack flag taped onto its paw. Iris prepared a celebratory lunch of offal and oatmeal, a concoction she had learned from "The Kitchen Front," a radio program that encouraged creative cookery with the use of rationed food items. This was followed by tinned fruit, a precious wartime commodity, after which they opened a long-hoarded bottle of gin. Their maid, Kate, dressed in an apron on her regular housework duties, came by and raised a glass with them.

The three later joined the throngs at Trafalgar Square, where people were jumping into the fountain and dancing on the pavement, and then made their way through the cheering crowds down the Mall toward Buckingham Palace, where the king and queen appeared with the two princesses and Prime Minister Churchill. As dusk fell, every light in London came on, and with the sky gradually darkening, public buildings were floodlighted. Forecasted rain stayed away. The evening was warm, spontaneous conga lines were formed, people waltzed in the streets, and soldiers swung from lampposts. Pubs were packed with people, but the three found a spot in the York Minster pub in Soho, where, according to Joan's diary, Caryll got tipsy on Pernod. Joan later reflected in her diary that Caryll, who had sometimes scared her, had "definitely mellowed a bit" over the course of the war.[5] As the night descended, there were fireworks and bonfires, and Caryll wrote to Maisie about the irony of the situation after a riotous day of rejoicing: "[I]t seemed not a little odd to us that human beings should find such delight in reproducing an imitation of the terrors we had at last done with!"[6]

The next night, Caryll and Iris went up to the roof of Nell Gwynn House where they had spent so many terrified nights as fire watchers, "but this time London was floodlit. I was so moved—like a child who suddenly wakes in the night to find her mother resplendent with jewels." From the roof, the city, which during the blackouts had been dark and desolate, "lay round us in [a] small ring, little dolls' houses and tiny spires and all the wounds and gaps visible." She added that looking down upon the churches, she realized "the tender love that has given Christ's body into man's keeping."[7]

Soon after V-E day, Caryll and Iris took a three-day holiday to Oxford, where they visited the Carmelite sisters. Caryll had become friends with the prioress ever since her talk there a year earlier. They again stayed at the Randolph Hotel (Caryll's friends would later make the observation that, oddly, whenever Caryll went away on a rare holiday, she insisted on staying at the best hotels.) V-J Day, August 13, meant that the world war was finally over. Caryll, however, was shocked that it took the massive destruction caused by an atomic bomb to bring about peace. She suggested to Henry that Catholics should plan a barefooted Tyburn walk[8] in reparation for the killing. There is no record that they did this walk.

Maisie's book with Caryll's prayers, called *The Splendour of the Rosary*, was published in 1945. The text begins with a thorough explanation of the rosary, its history, the theology behind it, and an instruction on how to use the rosary as a method of prayer, followed by a brief history of Fra Angelico and his paintings. The paintings are rendered in black and white, a choice that allowed the book to be affordable. For each decade of the rosary, beginning with the joyful mysteries, Maisie writes her own articulation of the picture that accompanies the decade. A scripture reading follows, accompanied by her own meditative commentary. Each decade ends with Caryll's prayer, simply titled "The Prayer." The words of the prayers are written in the form of "rhythms," the rhetorical form that Caryll had perfected ever since she had begun working for Father Bliss more than fifteen years earlier and that she had used in much of her work in the *Messenger of the Sacred Heart*. Repetitive and simple, the words of the prayers form a meditative incantation:

> Descend,
> Holy Spirit of Life!
> Come down into our hearts,
> That we may live.
> Descend into emptiness,
> That emptiness
> may be filled.

Descend into the dust,
that the dust may flower.
Descend into the dark,
that the light
may shine in darkness.[9]

Caryll's book, *The Flowering Tree*, was published a few months later. It is a series of meditations, once again in the form of rhythms. The meditations, many of which were first published in *The Grail*, have no clear organization. The book comprises reflections on gospel passages, such as the Sermon on the Mount, along with happenings in the course of Caryll's life: memories of "Soeur Marie Emilie," a lay sister at the Olton convent who sits shelling peas with gnarled fingers; certain points in the liturgical year, such as Holy Saturday; more recent happenings, such as the Blitz, or particular memories like that of a coffin in a church, or an afternoon in a cathedral. The meditations are intended to be read and prayed as one is conscious of one's breath. In an introduction, which is an excerpt from a letter to Maisie of August 31, 1944, Caryll describes the "secret of the wonderful power for peace in rhythmic prayer: finally just rhythmic breathing, which St. Ignatius proposes, and which was practised by Russian 'starets' long before St. Ignatius lived."[10] There is a flowing gentleness in the words of the text, which are intended to enter the reader's heart and be held in silent prayer. "The theme which recurs in them," Caryll writes in an author's note, "is the flowering of Christ in man."[11] One of the rhythms, "Philip Speaks," a several-page telling of the gospels according to the apostle Philip, had originally appeared in the September 1937 issue of *The Grail*. To her annoyance, *The Grail's* editors printed it again without her permission, along with the ongoing fiction that she was a member of their organization. At the time of its original appearance, John William Mackail, a distinguished Oxford academic and biographer of pre-Raphaelite artist and designer William Morris, had received permission to have separate copies of "Philip Speaks" printed, and had distributed them to friends. These friends included the poets

Laurence Banyon and John Masefield and novelist Dorothy Sayers, all of whom praised it as a new form of poetry.

Caryll continued to insist, however, that rhythms were not intended as poetry but as an entrée into contemplation. In *The Flowering Tree* a footnote to "Philip Speaks" reads: "Dedicated, in gratitude, to Dr. J.W. Mackail, O.M. in whose hands all that is good in 'Philip Speaks' has been multiplied."[12] It is probable that, despite her deep annoyance at *The Grail* for continuing to print her work, she was pleased that a whole sector of English literati with whom she was personally unacquainted admired it. The professor himself had just died before Caryll was able to put a copy of the book into his hands, but his widow, Margaret, who was the daughter of Edward Burne-Jones and the last of the children with memories of their pre-Raphaelite parents, invited Caryll to visit her. Caryll found the woman "serene and joyful, belonging to a different world. When you go into her home, it is as if you walked back into a different time, a time that is passed." She felt in the home a sorrow due to the man's recent death, "but sorrow completely transformed by dignity, and a serenity and joy."[13]

Now that the war was over, Frank Sheed, who had been traveling back and forth across the Atlantic, was finally able to return to England with his whole family. In April 1946, Frank, Maisie, and their children, Rosemary and Wilfred, arrived in London. At Caryll and Maisie's first face-to-face meeting, Maisie was shocked by "the dead-white face, the thick glasses, the fringe of red hair, a touch somehow of the grotesque—it was so surprising as to take one's breath away."[14]

Sixteen-year-old Wilfred Sheed, later to become a journalist and novelist, who walked with a brace as a result of polio, was told that Caryll compared him to "a field of golden corn struck down in its prime." He was determined to dislike anyone who spouted such pieties, and he wanted nothing to do with her. His terrible plight had captured Caryll's imagination, however, and she now offered to paint his portrait. The result of her artistic effort was not a success, but he later wrote: "[I]n no time I was posing for the sake of the conversation."

She proceeded to give Wilfred the full bohemian-Caryll treatment, complete with tales about her life of sin, gossip from her prewar days, and all kinds of magic-lantern entertainment, including stories about how she unearthed secrets with her psychic ability and handwriting knowledge, as well as "terrible and hilarious stories about her friends, [making] no attempt to love everybody." As a result, using "no special effects but her powdery face [she] managed to generate an *Arabian Nights* atmosphere in the engulfing grayness of 1946–7." It did not matter to him whether any of her stories were factually true. Unlike his parents, who "bought Caryll's whole catalog down to the last talking statue," Wilfred "both believed and didn't believe, as I suspect Caryll did and didn't." For the portrait sessions, he found Caryll "earthy, funny and rather creepily flattering." She laid the compliments thick, and he supposed the reason for them was because she felt he needed a boost of emotional support and self-confidence (she knew from Maisie that he was unhappy in his boarding school, Downside, where he would spend only a year). There may also have been something of the high emotive praise in her compliments that was reflected in her letters to Henry: another handsome young man in need of her help. In the end, for a teenager longing for his home back in the United States, "Caryll's prosaic manner and quirky imagination almost redeemed England" for Wilfred Sheed. His lasting impression, though, beneath the hilarity: "Being a saint would have cramped her style. Yet that she was one, I have no doubt. Her love of God was positively translucent."[15]

As Caryll's postwar life took shape, writing was at the forefront, with several important developments happening at the same time. She wrote to Henry that people were coming by in streams, as she was trying to work on yet another book, and she was serving tea to people ("friends," she puts in quotes) every day, unable to say no. Gert was pestering her "with a furious moan about neglecting and not loving my Mother."[16] Even the patient Iris was beginning to have frayed nerves. Iris was due to move her furniture into her empty cottage, and Caryll offered to help with the move. The cottage was a former shepherd's hut with a thatched roof and inside, a ladder that led to an attic. It remained empty after the purchase, but now Iris took steps to furnish it and made plans to live there part of the time while still maintaining her flat in London. Caryll helped her with the move, but the effort took planning and nego-tiating because the cottage stood in the middle of a field, and the work involved the pushing of a wheelbarrow to lug suitcases and other materials across an often muddy expanse.

Caryll at the cottage in the early 1950s. Iris's garden is in the background. Courtesy Camilla Shivarg.

To get to the cottage from London, one took a train to the town of Wendover and then a bus to the village of Terrick. The closest bus stop to Iris's cottage was still a quarter of a mile away. To reach the cottage, one then had to cross the field and climb over a stile. Caryll would eventually spend more and more time there, but she loved London, even in its postwar state of wreck-age and bombed-out buildings. Within the next few months, she would find another one-room flat, this one on the top floor of Nell Gwynn House, thus abandoning the first-floor "Kitch Morgue" (along with the ability to escape out the window when the inces-sant knocking on the door became too much). She was delighted with her new move: she now had a corner flat, with windows on both sides, giving a sense of light and air.

The year 1947 proved to be a watershed year for Caryll. On April 18, she had hernia surgery in Westminster Hospital. Five days later, still unable to sit up, she scrawled a note to Maisie in pencil, telling her that the operation "had to be twice as extensive as expected, but all the same I am recovering like wild fire."[17] In an unusual scene of family closeness, her mother picked her up at the hospital two weeks after the surgery and took her around to her father's, where they had tea. During her recuperation she was looked after by Iris in Iris's flat.

This medical milestone in her life was, in a sense, a harbinger. Friends would later remember that during the war Caryll ate very little, even though food, however unappetizing, was available at the First Aid Station, and during more normal times she was constantly entertaining friends at tea and supper although seemingly eating little herself. At some point during the war, her doctor ordered her to take two weeks off work because she was found to be anemic. In a letter a few years later she acknowledged that she tried starving herself as a young child, and again as an adolescent, perhaps as a reaction to an unhappy home life. Then there was the fasting she had attempted in her twenties, trying to emulate the saints, a hold on her that possibly never quite let go (two of her favorite saints, St. Catherine of Siena and St. Seraphim, fasted zealously). In the letter, written to a troubled friend who possibly had an eating disorder, she wrote of the effects of fasting: "lack of certain vitamins impairs the sight, in some cases causing temporary blindness. . . . This means that, although you can see in theory that it is desirable to be well, and right to try to get well, and though you really want to *want* to be well, you are not physically fit enough to be able to want it with your whole self."[18]

Her next book, a novel called *The Dry Wood*, was published a few months after her surgery. *The Dry Wood* is Caryll's only novel, but, she explained to a friend, "it is not the least bit a novel; it is really a spiritual book in the form of fiction."[19] The world she creates is, in a real sense, a fantasy. It also sheds light on Caryll herself, her view of the Catholic Church, its history, and her practical experience of it in the London of the 1930s and 1940s. The novel has the characteristics of popular fiction: a central story with a variety of characters and page-turning dialogue and suspense.

The event that sparks the action is the death of a parish priest, Father Malone, in a fictional part of London called Riverside. The local people consider Father Malone a saint and want to have his cause introduced. The miracle needed to ratify Father Malone's sanctity will be the healing of a young neighborhood child, Willie Jewel, who is dying. The whole parish then proceeds to pray a novena, asking God to heal the child through Father Malone's intercession. The characters that surround this central activity are all "types" of the Catholicism that swirled around Caryll and filled her life, and each represents a particular struggle in living the Christian life.

One of the most surprising elements is the presence of the Irish in her book—not surprising in one sense, because by necessity she rubbed shoulders with the Irish who had immigrated to England in droves over the previous century and who made up the bulk of the worshippers at most Catholic churches. But surprising in another sense, in that none of her friends were Irish, nor does she mention in her letters that she has had anything to do with Irish people in London. But in the novel, the Irish abound, from the dead priest himself, with his shabby hat and worn-down shoes and selfless ministry to the poor, to the tippling, kind-hearted Rose whose best days are behind her and who wears a once-elegant fur coat that has turned to mange. The matter-of-factness of a people steeped in the things of Catholicism is present in this world, as is discovered by an earnest young atheist who has decided to seek out a priest with the intention of converting: when the young man knocks at the door of the presbytery after having summoned the courage to approach it, the door is opened by "an apparition" who appears to be "someone between a policeman and a monk." The apparition greets him "almost menacingly":

"Can I see a priest?" Timothy said feebly.
"Which?"
"Anyone."

"They're at dinner."

"I could wait."

The apparition paused and peered down into Timothy's face. "I'm shortsighted," he said. "Are ye by any chance a sick call?"

"A what?"

"A sick call. Are ye in danger of death?"

"Oh, no—at least, I wasn't—"

"Well, that's a pity for ye. If ye were in danger of death, I could tell Father before the pudding."[20]

Caryll's savage humor comes through in every chapter, and the humor on the page is no doubt a reflection of the Caryll who held court at prewar parties as well as the postwar Caryll discovered by Wilfred Sheed. She clearly enjoys making a point of highlighting aspects of the Catholic Church that either amuse or bother her. The bad taste of church decoration: "Father O'Grady's church was a riot of vulgarity," she writes, and then describes the various statues around the church's interior: St. Thérèse of Lisieux (with "tears of real varnish on pallid cheeks"); St. Anthony of Padua ("with a sugar-mouse pink face of exquisite sweetness"); St. Aloysius Gonzaga ("so faint with prudery and anaemia that the lilies clasped to his breast might well have been there for his funeral."[21]) A framed picture of Pope Leo XIII, "looking very ill," is surrounded, "like satellites round their guiding star," by photographs of long-dead priests "painfully reminiscent of stuffed birds." And facing the Pope, "with a smile of almost brazen piety, considering the obvious licentiousness of her torturers, was a virgin martyr of the first century, who, like many a film star of our own days, had already been through fire and water without disarranging a single strand of her permanently waved hair."[22]

Cynical clergy make an appearance in *The Dry Wood*: the archbishop who peers out at the drab multitude on London's streets and decides that they need a saint; the monsignor whose cottage is the size of a mansion and whose wine cellar boasts only the finest. Caryll finds a way to insert members of the Grail in the book by creating the "Flames," a movement of fashionable young women embarking on apostolic work. A typical Flame possesses "good looks, good clothes, good health, good humour, and as much magnetism as one so free of any trace of neurosis could ever hope to have."[23]

If there is a hero in the novel, it is Father O'Grady, the successor as pastor of the sainted Father Malone. He tries, literally, to walk in the dead man's broken shoes. He stands between the greater men of the hierarchy and the simple folk of his parish, and he is a skeptic when it comes to miracles; true holiness, as he sees it, lies in the simplicity of the gospel. Spending dreary hours in the confessional, "he was glad that he had the cramp, the headache, the rheumatism and the nausea, because he had nothing else to offer in co-operation with God's huge intent of love."[24] As for Willie, the tiny child at the center of the hoped-for miracle, his parents were in wonder at the flicker of life "that could fight against the whole world and all its evil, and prevail in such weakness, such defencelessness, and such helplessness as this."[25]

The novel shows the breadth of Caryll's knowledge of Catholicism, including a strong hint of its historical dark underbelly. But her vision of the Church of the late 1940s is idealized, and the typical Irish Catholic churchgoer somewhat romanticized. Given her knowledge of the faith, and her insights into human nature, one wonders what her trenchant critiques might have looked like had she lived into and beyond the age of the Second Vatican Council.

As a work of fiction, *The Dry Wood* was generally reviewed unfavorably. *The Downside Review* claimed bluntly that "this is not a good novel," adding that "what thoughts the author has are so mistily expressed and so festooned with sentimentality as to produce no intellectual effect."[26] In the United States, the reviewer in *The Sewanee Review* claimed that "the recurring platitudes . . . have the effect of interfering with any poetic grace; and in addition, stop the narrative and put the author on the stage at too frequent intervals and for too long a time."[27] The same issue of *The Sewanee Review* also published a piece of fiction called "The

Train," by a twenty-three-year-old American writer by the name of Flannery O'Connor, featuring a character called Haze, who, in a later iteration—the novel *Wise Blood*—would found a "Church Without Christ" which would eventually lead him to Christ. In a literary what-might-have-been, what would the meeting have been like of these two women writers, each strange and even "grotesque" in her own way, and each seeking God via the Cross and through the written word?

Another book, *The Comforting of Christ*, was published the same year. The title page describes it as "a Peace-Time Edition Revised and Enlarged of *This War Is the Passion*." Most of the original book is left, with only the "this war" parts—which had given the original book its potent immediacy—taken out. Replacing these parts are anecdotes of the war brought in to make a point—for example, the sight of a small boy in church who laughed with delight at the quivering of a flower caused by a flying bomb as the adults around him quaked. To "The Defences of the Mind," Caryll adds a third defense: dealing with fear. She also adds a whole section she calls "Reparation." The overall result of the book is that the added parts tend to be worked over and are less immediate, less direct, thus lacking the gasp-in-the-throat recognition of her wartime thoughts. But it retains the same tone of authority and confidence in the spiritual message. Commenting on a general tendency to retreat into selfishness after years of contributing to the war effort, Caryll writes how "it is part of our instinct to shrink to the size of self instead of expanding to the size of Christ." She continues, "But our wholeness is bigger than the world, bigger than humanity: we are part of the whole Christ."[28]

A postwar activity that Caryll had been planning with Archie Campbell-Murdoch, based on a suggestion made by Dr. Strauss, came to fruition in 1947. This was a school for so-called "backward" boys—not only boys with learning disabilities, but also youngsters who had been traumatized by bombing as well as young refugees who had witnessed the war firsthand. Archie became the head-master, and the school, named for St. Thomas More, was located in Frensham, a village in Surrey. Caryll was hired for one day a week to give lessons in art to the four classes in which the boys had been placed. Every Tuesday she took the hour-long train ride to the nearby station in Farnham, where Archie met her. Her letters during the autumn of 1947 (and even well into the following two years) are full of plans and ideas: suggestions for the purchase of wood and other construction materials so that toys could be made; ideas for combining art lessons with music and drama; thoughts on the teaching of liturgical art; advice on the size of classes; plans for structuring the lessons and the purchasing of poster paper, brushes, pencils, pens, and so on. And then her philosophy of the teaching of art: "In a word, art must be gradually understood in its relation to ordinary life, and to all sorts of other things that are learnt in school. . . . If some don't actually draw at all it won't matter, so long as they come to realize the effect of art on life."[29]

In a letter of September 25, 1947, she informed Archie of an upcoming event: Joan Wyndham, now twenty-six, demobilized and enrolled in a secretarial course in Oxford, had announced that she was married and was about to have a baby. The baby's father was an Oxford student by the name of Maurice Rowden. Since Joan was still in studies, a plan was developed in which the baby would spend weekdays with Iris, having Caryll's help, and with the baby's parents on the weekends. At first Caryll did not like the idea: she resented anything that got in the way of her writing—and besides, she knew nothing about babies, having scant experience of them herself, even though there are letters indicating the devotion she felt to the children in her life: David Billaux and her two nieces, to whom she periodically sent postcards from the teddy bear, Roosy, written in a childish Cockney style, when they were children.

Joan's daughter was born in November and was named Clare. Having a baby to help look after brought a new dimension to Caryll's life, and she soon discovered that her lack of knowledge when it came to the needs of infants did not matter. She and Iris—whose ignorance in that regard was little less than Caryll's, because as a high-born young mother she had had a nanny to see to the child's physical needs—quickly learned together. During these postwar years, however, Caryll was kept busy with other things: people still clamoring to speak to her, inviting her to tea, encroaching on her writing time.

Early in 1948, she enlisted Henry to accompany her to a cocktail party to celebrate the silver wedding anniversary of her sister Ruth and her husband. Apart from that event, her social calendar revolved around her own circle of friends, and it included the "Loaves and Fishes." This group, during the war, tried as much as possible to continue helping the "Sea-horses," the one-time well-off people within their orbit who needed financial help. That need increased when postwar austerities were affecting everyone. Caryll's letters speak of how busy and exhausted she is, even as she is issuing invitations to tea and supper, making arrangements, and finding help for the Sea-horses, who were often lonely and elderly people, and "very often people who are always on the lookout for slights, fearfully self-deluded, and almost impossible to get on with."[30] One of the Sea-horses, a woman she names "Dodo," she finds downright irritating.

Her carving continues: she writes in one letter that she is putting the finishing touches on a set of Stations of the Cross for Grossé. In letters to Henry she writes of her toothaches and exhaustion: she is already tired when she wakes up in the morning. She admits crankiness toward her long-time champion, Father Bliss. On April 11, 1948, she writes to Henry that she has scrapped a plan to invite Father Bliss to her flat (the Jesuit had long since recognized Caryll's unique spiritual gifts and had taken to bringing friends to meet her—on this occasion it was to be the former Member of Parliament, Leslie Hore-Belisha): "I would not for the whole world have him know it, but to me he [Father Bliss] is very exhausting. He usually ends up by coming to lunch as well, and one can't rely on him not bringing more and more friends, and it is very difficult to make him hear what I say. I always think he is going to fall down, or that he wants to pee!"[31]

A few weeks later, she received the news that her other Jesuit guide, Father Steuart, who spent the war years as superior at the Mount Street community in London before retiring to Wimbledon, had, at the age of seventy-four, a series of debilitating strokes. And then, on July 14 she wrote to Maisie: "Doubtless you know of dear old Father Steuart having died last Friday. I'm glad he did not live on after the stroke as he had lost his speech and did not know anyone."[32]

Important deaths would continue to take place. In February 1949, Caryll kept Henry apprised of the decline of her beloved cat, Jones. On February 18, she wrote to say that she had had him put down: "[T]he only thing I could do, to be fair to the most lovely, innocent old friend I have ever had was to prevent suffering for him."[33]

Letters kept arriving from readers asking her advice. The pile never seemed to diminish. Often, she agreed to meet the letter-writers personally in what had now become a free consultation service. She liked to have Archie's boys to tea and to give them extra carving lessons, but there were too many things and people crowding her day, and she was overwhelmed all the time. She told one correspondent that her sleep was down to four hours a night so that she could get all of her work done. The result was depression and self-recrimination, and the recipients of her distressed cry were Maisie and Frank, with whom she continued to compare herself unfavorably. In her imagination, the books she was planning to write were magnificent, but when she put pen to paper, they became "unmanageable little miseries."[34] Her next book was going to be "a little maggot" compared with the large and impressive books that the Sheeds, between them, produced. Maisie's book, *Young Mr. Newman*, about the early life of John Henry Newman, running at over four hundred pages, had just been published, as if to confirm Caryll's depressed sense of her own upcoming effort.

Caryll's next book, *The Passion of the Infant Christ*, was published in 1949. She told friends that the idea for it began early in the war, when she spent her first night in the rat-infested basement of the First Aid Post. She thought of King Herod and the innocent infants

in Bethlehem he was determined to kill. Every chapter is complete
in itself and the chapters may have been written at different times
over the previous few years and brought together and expanded
when an actual infant, in the person of Iris's granddaughter, Clare,
came into Caryll's life. The theme throughout (although she tends
to wander with this) is the presence of Calvary in Bethlehem; the
seed must fall into the earth and die in order for new life to be
born. As usual with her work, the writing is at its best when fresh
insight is distilled, often into a single sentence, as if she were a
sage of old who has spent years on the mountaintop pondering
the meaning of the Christian life. In the words of the review of
the book in *America* magazine, "Several of her paragraphs, though
somewhat detached from the main theme, stand by themselves as
little masterpieces, blossom-like miniatures of ascetical teaching."[35]

Her writing grabs the reader most when her pen stays down to
earth. A few passages in *The Passion of the Infant Christ*, such as
the picture of "a child asleep in his mother's arms,"[36] tend to slide
into the romantic and sentimental, but then the clear-eyed Caryll
emerges again with a fresh look at the Christ of the gospels—even
on the next page: "As we look at the world today, it is not easy to
believe that everywhere Christ is born again, that God looks down
on the wreckage and misery, the fiasco if you like, that we have
made of the world, and seeing us in the midst of it says, 'This is
my well-beloved Son!'"[37]

The reviewer in *Life of the Spirit* made the connection between
the text of *The Passion of the Infant Christ* and Christ's injunction
to become like little children: "[W]e must ever retain something
of the simplicity, innocence, spontaneity, generosity, docility of the
child."[38] The presentation of Christ as an infant has a rich tradition dating back to the early Church, but a few within Caryll's
circle thought that sentimentality—perhaps a holdover from the
Victorian language that Caryll inherited—marred some of Caryll's
work. Wilfred Sheed, while admiring Caryll immensely, wrote,
"Her published essays and verse could be tender to the verge of
soupy."[39] And her friend Dickie Orpen, a few years earlier, turned

down the introduction Caryll had written to her book, *Meditations with a Pencil* (a series of drawings illustrating gospel passages), because she thought Caryll's language too saccharine, even while aware that the name of Caryll Houselander on the cover would have brought more sales to her work.

Letters to Archie during the late 1940s indicate that all is not well with Caryll's health. She has to miss school for this and that reason: a sore throat, a high temperature, a possible infection. A gastric attack. Trouble with her teeth. Her letters are still full of ideas and suggestions, however, and she is obviously very involved in the life of the school: some boys do not like art and prefer to study bookbinding instead; some of the classes are too big and should be divided, she writes, and a detailed suggestion follows on how this division should come about, with the boys' names in two lists.

Then, in a letter of March 19, 1949: the gastric attack of an earlier letter turns out to be something more serious and long-lasting and has proved to be the real cause of the hernia surgery of two years earlier. She does not specify what the condition is. She writes that, according to her doctor, this condition is also the cause of the extreme fatigue she feels constantly. She must therefore stop teaching at Archie's school on a regular basis, and yet even as she writes this, she continues with plans and suggestions on how her work with the boys can continue without her. She had been inviting some of them in small groups to Iris's cottage during the summer holidays, and says she will continue to do so.

Creative ideas continued despite her ill health and exhaustion: Could the boys be taught how to make puppets? Might simple trades be taught in order to give the boys practical skills for work in the future? Caryll already had Maisie involved in the school's welfare: the Sheeds had bought a farm in Essex after their return to England, and Maisie regularly sent food from the farm to the school as well as wood for carving and cardboard for bookbinding. Caryll sought Archie's assistance in finding work at the school for a Polish refugee whom Maisie was trying to help; Maisie had a particular interest in helping Polish refugees because she believed that England had defaulted on its responsibilities to Poland at the start of the war. Likewise, help for the Sea-horses, still suffering from the postwar austerities, was sought from Maisie, who had sent Caryll parcels of food during the war and now agreed to help out those within Caryll's circle who were in need. Best of all, as far as the school was concerned—"a grand bit of news"—Caryll was able to get Maisie involved in fundraising: "[S]he is all out to take it under her wing, and to go round and collect money for the building of good recreation and class rooms herself. She is also ready to give a substantial donation herself. Maisie is very outspoken and to put it mildly, tactless—but she is a darling, the straightest and kindest of women and with *tremendous* influence."[40]

In a further letter, clearly saddened by her decision to no longer teach at Archie's school, Caryll writes that she has never had "the skill that could make my dreams become reality. I am by nature a person to start things, to sow seeds as it were; it requires others to see them through."[41] Her artistic talent, however, remained at the school in the form of the Stations of the Cross she had carved for the school's chapel. The chapel and the Stations would eventually be destroyed by fire some years later.

Her energy was now so depleted she was relying on the energy-boosting (and addictive) drug Benzedrine to get through the day. In a letter to Henry she says she "greatly want[s] Benzedrine, or Dexedrine, which I am told is much the same and easier to get."[42] She was going to try and get it herself, she writes, but if not, she was relying on someone called "John" to obtain it for her. And in a letter a few weeks later, she is "a thousand times" grateful to John for getting her the Benzadrine: "it is more and more required."[43]

At the end of the summer of 1949, Caryll, Iris, and Henry made the twelve-mile pilgrimage from Cambridge to the ancient shrine of Our Lady of Walsingham, in Norfolk, where the Virgin Mary was said to have appeared in the eleventh century. At Cambridge, they stayed at the Blue Boar Hotel (Caryll once again insisting that she stay in the best hotel and that the room be inspected for mice). She and Iris decided to walk the final mile, known as the Holy

Mile, in the time-honored penitential tradition of approaching the shrine on bare feet. Having already walked some distance along the Holy Mile, their shoes slung around their necks, however, they came upon a sign that read, "To Walsingham, 1 mile." The humor of the situation was the final memory of the solemn pilgrimage.

As the 1940s drew to a close, Caryll wrote in a late December letter to Archie that she was now feeling well. She was longing to return to the school and hoped she could soon work there again, perhaps as an assistant to the teacher who had replaced her. In the meantime, she was again working on a new book, "which I have been struggling to finish for nearly two years."[44]

Caryll and Iris on pilgrimage to Walsingham, 1948. Courtesy Camilla Shivarg.

7

Final Journey
(1950–1954)

And God accepted the offering; the fragments of love were gathered up into the wholeness of Love and nothing was wasted.

—The Dry Wood

Soon after the new decade of the 1950s began, Caryll came down with pneumonia. Complete rest for a month was ordered, no visitors allowed, and for her the solitude became like a spiritual retreat. From her corner flat at the top of Nell Gwynn House, she could see the Brompton Oratory and hear the ringing of the Angelus three times a day, as well as the Sanctus bell during Mass. She wrote to Maisie that she felt surrounded by God's presence.

It was not an entirely peaceful recovery period, however. Iris looked after her during her convalescence, but Iris herself was suffering from rheumatic pain and hobbled around as Caryll lay bedridden. It was a recurring phenomenon throughout their years of living together. Whenever Caryll got sick, Iris tended to her care, but then soon, Iris too became sick and suggested in so many words that it was Caryll's illness that had brought about her own, or that she had been sick all along while looking after Caryll.

The result now was that "it has brought on fearful guilt and she is now simply obsessed by her pain and suffering and the usual story of having hidden it from my unseeing eyes," Caryll wrote to Henry. "So I just can't go on lying in bed half the day and keeping up my own delicate state as I would like to do. For me to be ill is as certain to produce an attack of something acutely painful for Iris, as it would be if I simply handed her out a dose of poison!"

Her mother, too, was in a state of misery and cast her own anxieties upon Caryll: "Gert has paid me several visits and talked all the time of her own illnesses and grievances." Inflammation remained in one of Caryll's lungs, and her labored breathing drained her of all energy. As a result, it was a dark period for her, and she confided to Henry that she had never enjoyed the talents she had been given because "they have always been violated, scamped, hurried, fitted in to other people's convenience and never allowed to grow."[1]

When the month was over, she remained an outpatient of the Brompton Chest Hospital, but still had little energy. Iris's physical complaints had lightened, but her nerves were suffering, and she was on medication for anxiety. Given the rundown state of both of them, Caryll felt herself "in such a state of general anxiety . . . that I can hardly distinguish between real and imaginary things."[2] All the same, she was once again entertaining friends for lunch or tea in the Nell Gwynn House Restaurant, preceded by a glass of sherry in her flat.

Since the end of the war, Iris had become increasingly attached to her cottage and had discovered that she loved gardening. Eventually, her garden began to flourish. A small stream ran through it, enhancing its serene beauty, and every year in the spring the cottage became her home, until cool weather forced her back to London as winter approached. Caryll was a diehard Londoner, but by this time in their lives neither was able to live comfortably without the other; despite disagreements and quarreling, Caryll spent part of the summer and fall at the cottage as well, despite the inconvenience of having to cross an often muddy field to get anywhere (including the post box). In letters written at the cottage, she gave as her quaint return address "The Thatched Cottage, Nash Lea Farm, Terrick, Nr Aylesbury, Bucks." She and Iris had a simple routine: daily Mass in the town of Princes Risborough, a quarter of a mile to the bus and four miles by bus to the town. Sometimes they cycled to the early Mass in Wendover, which was closer, but which had no bus connection to anywhere near the cottage. The rest of the day Caryll was free to write, with Iris calling her only for meals. Iris managed the upkeep of the cottage herself.

Among the advantages to the cottage was that its relative remoteness meant people seeking Caryll's help were unable to find her; she could write without interruption. By now, she had a number of writing projects on the go. Besides book manuscripts, there were articles. Ever since she had been discovered by the North American Catholic reading public, editors sought her work. She rarely said no. Frank Sheed himself, knowing the value of her name, asked her to write the foreword to a book called *Reproachfully Yours* by an American author, Lucile Hasley, with whom Caryll had been corresponding. Due to the publisher's time constraints, the text of the book was unavailable to her, but she had read Lucile Hasley's work before and was aware of the other writer's style, which was to treat difficult matters with a light and cheerful touch. Blindly enthusing over a book she had not yet read, Caryll managed to cover two pages with admirable filler: "Lucile Hasley's writing . . . gives her laughter and intense realism that essential quality which makes her words come alive and go home to us, home to our minds and to our hearts, and home to stay."[3]

On November 13, 1950, Gert Houselander died at the age of seventy-five in a public ward in St. George's Hospital. She was found to have breast cancer two years previously and her right breast had been surgically removed. Caryll and Ruth kept constant vigil at her deathbed, sleeping slumped down in their chairs and reviving themselves with a bottle of brandy, which they passed back and forth. Gert had been given a minimum of morphine to ease her pain, and death came slowly. Six months before her death she had been reading a book called *Odette*, about a Catholic spy who had been imprisoned during the recent war, and the woman's story had "pierced her pitiful armour and made her feel ashamed of self pity."[4] Still, Caryll claimed that the brashness that had been a central feature in her mother's personality accompanied her in her final illness, along with resentment over the fate ahead of her, but upon receiving the last rites a week before her death, "she became peaceful and gentle as I had never known her in life—everything harsh and difficult seemed to be wiped away."[5] Gert and Willmott carried on their friendly enmity over the decades, and when Willmott retired from banking fifteen years earlier and moved to London, the two remained in touch in the face of each other's needs, meeting almost daily in the latter years. After Gert's funeral, he said to Caryll: "She was an old b____, but God, how we shall miss her!"[6]

By early 1951, the manuscript of Caryll's next book, which was to be called *Guilt*, and which she had been working on since at least the middle years of the war, reached the publisher. It was out of her hands. The relief of this unburdening of herself may partly explain the somber but unharried tone of her news in a letter of March 27, 1951, to Archie: "I have a rather big pill to swallow and need your prayers." Less than five months after her mother's death, the news was that both her doctor and a surgeon who had been consulted thought that a tumor in her left breast was cancerous. If there was any good in the terrible news, it was that both doctors agreed that the tumor was probably in the early stage, and so if it proved to be malignant, was likely curable with the removal of the breast followed by radium treatment. In the same letter, she went on lightheartedly to write that when all was over and she had returned home from the hospital, they would "refresh" their souls "on theology and Tio Pepe."[7]

She was admitted to Westminster Hospital on March 30 and surgery took place on April 9. During the intervening ten days she received a series of radiation treatments which, she told Maisie, were intended to shrink the tumor and limit the area of the surgery. In the meantime, the general hospital ward became her universe. She dreaded being a patient in a general ward, having little privacy, but the experience buoyed her and perhaps even allowed her to forget the seriousness of the situation. She picked up the medical jargon and used it to banter with the hospital staff and other patients. Between treatments, she enjoyed the goings-on of the ward, taking an interest in the modern equipment, helping wash teacups, talking with the other patients and zeroing in on those who were Catholics, gently edging her way into suggesting to some that their physical woes were a participation in Christ's suffering. In a later letter she indicated disgust for the Catholic priests who came to minister to the patients, saying they cared only for saving souls and seemed tongue-tied when it came to showing empathy or kindness: "[O]ne has the impression that they must send ones who are too stupid for jobs they think more worth while." But the hospital staff held her admiration, as did her fellow patients: "The real charity and courage of human beings is manifest here, even more than it was in war-time," she wrote to a friend, "probably because there is more humility."[8]

During the period before surgery, she was also used as a medical specimen for a group of doctors who were learning to specialize as surgeons. Without emotion she told Maisie that when asked about her prognosis, they evaded her questions, but the teaching doctor, speaking to the students about the human specimen before them, offered his unvarnished opinion: "[F]rom what he said, my chances seemed pretty poor."[9] But she was pleased to add that the radiologist seemed genuinely thrilled to report that the treatment was successful beyond all expectation.

Three weeks later, in a long letter to Frank and Maisie she said that the surgery—a mastectomy of her left breast—was a success, but the wound had become infected and she had been given opium to blunt the pain. And "success" was a vague enough word to sidestep the meaning of the actual prognosis and the chance that the cancer might recur. In another letter she wrote that the result of the surgery was fifty-fifty, with chances on the downside. In a burst of dark humor she repeated verbatim what the "guinea pig" doctor, "a great man on cancer cure," had said: "I was 'a most beautiful example of malignant cancer.'"[10]

Her six-week recovery period in the hospital brought with it other headaches. Friends insisted on coming to visit, and she complained that invariably people who had little to do with each other would visit at the same time. Only two visitors at once were allowed, and it was up to the exhausted patient to decide which two were to stay and which were to be left standing outside in the passageway. Even then, sometimes the two did not necessarily know each other, and it was up to her to make small talk with them. Before the surgery, Caryll had named Iris as next of kin, whereupon Iris, realizing this, had a nervous collapse and blamed Caryll. In her letter to Archie, Caryll wrote: "Please say a prayer for me and for poor old Iris who is more upset than I am. I haven't told her they think it is cancer; in fact, despite Cardinal Newman's opinion that it is better for the whole race to be destroyed than one venial sin be committed, I have sinned to the extent of telling her a lie."[11]

Iris, in the face of her own fragile nervous state, left for the cottage before Caryll's surgery, and thus was not with her during this period. To Maisie, Caryll wrote: "I shall feel terribly sad if I have to have the operation with her out of reach—but then I don't think she could stand being in the hospital, and in any case I would feel desperately guilty if I imposed yet more suffering on her. I feel dreadfully guilty as it is."[12] With Dickie, she was more candid about her emotional state in the face of Iris's reaction: "I need not tell you . . . that this fact has opened such a vast chasm of loneliness before me as I have never known before; but I am telling myself that Christ's beloved Peter left Him, out of weakness, when he most needed him; and I am really not worthy to share even as remotely as this in Christ's suffering."

In the same letter, she wrote that she spent the long night hours trying to pray, telling herself that she was in God's hands, that "it is not only my wretched body and shivering soul that I am at last committing absolutely to the hands of Infinite Love but . . . all those whom I love." She was under little illusion, she told Dickie, despite her friends' assurances that women they knew came through such surgery with flying colors, "I know only two people who have had 'the same': my mother, whom I have lately seen die in agony, and a friend who is living but has been told, a year ago, that two years is the very utmost she can expect."[13] Several years later, recalling Caryll's anguish at this crucial moment, Dickie wrote to Maisie Ward: "Caryll at that time was quite desolated by Iris's collapse. It seemed then to me like the candles going out at Tenebrae."[14] If there was any consolation for Caryll during this period, it was that by the time she left the hospital, two night nurses and the house surgeon, Dr. Douglas Begg, had become friends and would eventually be invited to visit her at the cottage.

Caryll went home to Nell Gwynn House after her hospital stay, returning every day for five weeks for "deep ray treatment," which exhausted her. Her orders were for complete rest, but friends and acquaintances at once began to come around to see her. Compounding the pain and exhaustion was the situation of her father: now in his eighties, he had felt bereft by Gert's death, and Caryll feared that her own surgery, exactly like her mother's and coming so soon after her death, would be too much for him. She minimized the importance of the surgery, and so felt that she must resume her visits to him and continue to act as if she returned to perfect health. By early July, she was back at the cottage with Iris. Soon afterward, Caryll's father joined them there and stayed for two weeks. Although having invited him, Caryll dreaded the visit, but to her relief he took an avid interest in the garden and spent most of the time outdoors with Iris, advising her on the pruning of roses.

Guilt made little fanfare when it was published in 1952, and its appearance after traumatic surgery may have been an anticlimax, but Caryll considered it her most important book. Some of her letters to Maisie were attempts at working out her thoughts and ideas for the book. She visited the Hanwell Insane Asylum, also known as St. Bernard's Hospital, as part of her research, and wrote to both Henry and Frank about her experiences there, indicating she learned more about love and evil in that place of pain than she could have learned anywhere else: "[Y]ou've just got the world, unmasked, unbandaged, in its essence, before your eyes," she wrote.[15]

In the book's introduction, Caryll uses the hyphenated word "ego-neurosis" to identify a form of spiritual suffering she sees around her, and so from the beginning, "guilt" is used within a religious context. This is fleshed out further in the introductory sentence to the chapter called "Mechanisms of Escape": "Modern man, having succeeded in blinding himself to the reality of guilt, and lost or numbed his sense of sin, is intent upon ridding himself of the misplaced *feeling* of guilt."[16] She quotes the expert whom she describes as the greatest of all psychologists, C. G. Jung, in claiming this phenomenon as an illness of the soul. It is manifest in a general dissatisfaction and shame in simply being oneself. This "disease in man's soul"[17] causes inner pain. She tells readers that she is offering her theories to others in the hope that as a result of her own ego-neurosis they may know at least a modicum of happiness. As if giving a clue, she lets readers know that she is writing the introduction on the Feast of Our Lady of Sorrows (in 1950).

The text of the book itself begins with a quote from Julian of Norwich—a suggestion from the beginning that the author is searching for Christian wisdom on behalf of herself and her readers:

> In nature we have our being
> In mercy we have our increasing
> In grace we have our fulfilling.

She writes with authority, in short, declarative sentences, and there are often flashes of brief, passionate bursts of insight. She is like a sage in places, as if long-practiced in the scholarly study of her subject. There is no acknowledgment of her lack of formal background in the study of psychology: the omission suggests that she is letting the reader know that she has read and assimilated material written by better educated minds than hers, and that she considers this to be sufficient when combined with her own perception and her deep reading of scripture.

Here is Caryll telling her reader that psychological suffering was the immediate effect of the first sin: "In the penetrating light of

God, self-knowledge became unbearable to Adam."[18] As a result of this first sin, she goes on, humanity has "a double obligation": "both to accept suffering and to wrestle with it." She explains a few paragraphs further: in light of Adam's sin, "we are obliged as human creatures to accept the common lot," and again: "To regard ourselves as exceptions, somehow exempt from the common lot of fallen men, is to attempt to separate ourselves from humanity." Even further: in light of Christ's suffering and death, we have "a transfiguration of sorrow."[19]

Although Caryll's context is clearly Christian from the first page, she only gradually introduces the Christ-life. It is mainly in the chapter called "Christ and Guilt" where the reader is the beneficiary of Caryll's deep reading of the gospels. She writes: "In Gethsemane Christ faced the crisis which so many millions must face when they are challenged by love—will they be stripped of all pretence, and be naked, themselves, before love?"[20] As in *This War Is the Passion* and other earlier books, there is a profound knowledge of scripture, and the reader can only gasp at the simple, clear truth of what she writes. In the second half of the book, we find robust descriptions of how Christ worked in the lives of neurotic saints. In the case of the "very sentimental little French bourgeoise" who became the rose-petal saint, Thérèse of Lisieux, the elements of her personality and her day-to-day actions tell us not so much what they reveal about the saint herself, "but what they tell us about Christ. Not that Teresa wants to become Christ, but that Christ wills to become Teresa."[21]

The book, on the whole, is uneven: parts of it could have been written with the biblical insights of the twenty-first century. Other parts—sections on the "causes" of homosexuality and the denigrating of Protestantism—reflect the narrow Catholic views of the mid-twentieth century.

Guilt received mixed critical reviews. The American Catholic monthly periodical *Integrity* described it as offering "the vision of a world entering with Christ into the Garden of Gethsemane." The reviewer added, "It is diffuse and rambling—but shocking, charged as it is with the electricity of truth."[22] The problem with the message, the reviewer goes on to say, is the question of "how to become willing to suffer when we aren't willing, in order to be able to love when we can't love, in order to come closer to wholeness and God. Miss Houselander is not very successful in getting us off—not because she doesn't have the solution, but because it gets lost in the diffuseness and disclarity of the book."[23] A review in *Renascence* referred to this diffuseness as "dartings about" and then made the perceptive comment that "all the concern with guilt and its endless ramifications was only the backdrop to something else. . . . The book is a prose hymn to saintliness and the saints, and of course, the One in whom the saints coinhere. The taste of holiness is strong here, sharp and pungent."[24]

The *Catholic Times* made the tepid comment that the wide ground covered in *Guilt* includes "a number of personal and debatable opinions."[25] Indeed, Sheed & Ward ran into difficulty in obtaining the imprimatur for the book from the cardinal-archbishop's office in New York, and so the publisher took it to the Boston archdiocese. Thus the book contains the imprimatur of Archbishop (later Cardinal) Richard J. Cushing of Boston, and an unusual statement appears on the same page, perhaps in the subtle form of a caveat. It reads: "The Nihil Obstat and the Imprimatur are ecclesiastical declarations that a publication is free of doctrinal or moral error, not a statement of the positive worth, nor an implication that the contents have the Archbishop's approval or recommendation."[26] Maisie Ward, however, learned something more down-to-earth from *Guilt*: "that the difference between neurotic and normal in our shared human nature is more one of degree than of kind, that we can all learn profitably the lesson of how to deal with unhealthy moods and unreasonable fancies."[27] *Guilt* would be Caryll's last book published in her lifetime.

There was considerable activity at the cottage during the summer of 1952. Joan, who had been living in Baghdad where her husband was teaching, returned to England with Clare. She was now divorced and married to Shura Shivarg and was again expecting a baby. Clare stayed at the cottage for much of the summer with Iris and Caryll. Caryll's mother had left her a modest sum of money in her will, and between them, Iris and Caryll decided that Caryll should have a separate building as a studio and a place to invite guests. Iris gave her a small plot of land on the property, and blueprints were drawn up and sent away for approval. Matters were stalled, however, because postwar shortage of building materials was still in effect and endless regulations had to be met. In the end, a pre-fabricated hut was purchased, and the summer weeks were spent fixing it up. In odd moments, Caryll carved and chiseled, using branches from trees around the property. One day a neighboring farmer told Caryll that the sound of her chiseling, which carried across the field, reminded him of the tapping of a woodpecker, and so Caryll decided to call the hut Woodpeckers.

The small building contained a main room with Caryll's workbench, a small bedroom, and a tiny room with a toilet and sink. Caryll decided from the beginning that furnishings would be kept to a minimum. Like the garden shed from years earlier at Milborne Grove, Woodpeckers was kept clean and without clutter. Friends marveled at the fairy-tale quality of the miniature home. As usual, Caryll kept her materials neat and immaculate. She had with her only the books that she needed for whatever writing she was doing. When she finished with them, she returned them to her London flat.

One of her summer visitors was Yvonne Bosch van Drakestein. When news of Caryll's surgery reached her more than a year earlier, Yvonne had sent flowers to the hospital and received a long letter of thanks. It had been almost ten years since their last communication, and in the meantime the English Grail had separated from the international movement and remained under Yvonne's direction. There had been no personal rancor between the two women, and if it took effort on Caryll's part to maintain a loving attitude to Yvonne, no record of such effort exists.[28] In a letter expressing delight in receiving the flowers, she wrote, "[H]ow often, indeed daily and nightly, I have thought of you and prayed for you, and I never have ceased to love you and never shall."[29]

Another visitor was a woman by the name of Odette Churchill. As a French-born married woman with three daughters, Odette Sansom (as her married name was at the time) had been recruited by the Special Operations Executive in 1942 to do undercover work in Nazi-occupied France. In 1943 she was captured, interrogated, and tortured by the Gestapo in Fresnes Prison, near Paris. She was condemned to be executed, but instead was sent to Ravensbrück concentration camp, where she was held in solitary confinement and fed starvation rations. She later received the George Cross for her bravery. After the war she said that her faith and the Catholic devotions she had learned from childhood kept her going in her lowest moments. A biography of Odette (the book that had so impressed Gert Houselander) was written soon after the war, and in 1950 a film, *Odette*, was released.

Frank Sheed was taken with Odette's story and suggested that Caryll write a short book highlighting Odette's bravery and prison trials, infused with the faith and devotions that sustained her during interrogation and prison. The book would also be the answer to hundreds of letters the former prisoner had received asking her questions about how she dealt with fear and hatred and torture and what her attitude now was toward her enemies. In Caryll's mind the answer would be love. The three had lunch together, and Caryll invited Odette to the cottage. The film about Odette had recently played in Aylesbury, and when people in the area got wind of her presence, a small crowd appeared at the gate. Odette spent two days at the cottage and allowed Caryll to hold the worn little prayer book that had helped sustain her in the concentration camp. In the end, the biographical project was abandoned. After the war, Odette had divorced her husband and married Peter Churchill, a fellow spy she met in France. Either Caryll or Frank—or perhaps both—realized the difficulty in trying to build up a woman with a couple of living husbands into a Catholic heroine. In a few years Odette would divorce and re-marry again and become Odette Hallows.

Another death took place that summer. Father Bliss had been diagnosed with throat cancer two years earlier and had relied on

Caryll for moral support. He resigned, perhaps reluctantly, from his editorial duties, and, with time on his hands, sent her many letters expressing a wish to come to lunch, and then stayed on and on for tea. She came to dread the visits because of the emotional toll it took on her to see him in his lonely state, with death ahead of him. In early January 1951, she told friends she hoped he would die soon, but he did not die until August 4, 1952, at St. Anthony's Hospital in Cheam, just outside London. His death came as a relief, but it marked the end of an era for Caryll. In many ways their relationship had become reversed: Caryll, the employee who had been desperate for work and spiritual help thirty years earlier, had become the mother helper to her former mentor. Her letters referring to Father Bliss's visits during these last years reflect a depleted sensibility, and she always sought the help of Henry Tayler to ease the emotional burden the Jesuit's visits brought to her.

By early 1953, she was feeling generally unwell, sometimes thinking that she had influenza, at other times that she had a case of "nerves." She was getting checkups every two months, and each time, she told friends she had received a good report of health. Friends would remember how, as her health declined further, Caryll's patience also declined—how, even in her cozy haven, Woodpeckers, she would say how much she hated being in the country, how she could not put up with So-and-so's mawkishness, and so on. There was now a tendency to be upset easily by people who, at another time, she not only put up with but regarded with tenderness and love. And now a new phenomenon: inability to sleep. Unlike former times when she would get out of bed and write whenever she was afflicted with occasional insomnia, she now found she did not have the energy to get up at all. And so, when she woke at four o'clock in the morning, she tried to pray for her friends.

It is difficult to know how much Caryll knew about her medical prognosis and how much she wrote optimistic letters because she did not want her friends, especially Iris, to worry. Dickie Orpen, with whom Caryll seemed to be more candid than she was with some other friends, wrote several years later that "I never knew whether she believed or only wanted to believe the drivel the doctor talked. She told me on the telephone that she had said to the doctor, 'but I am dying,' and he had told her that was pure neurosis plus a few swollen glands."[30] She also tried to return to a normal life of helping others, as if she were of robust health. This effort included going to court with a friend who was being sued by her former husband. She wrote chirpy letters to Dr. Begg, who, surely, having become a friend (by now she had become on a first-name basis with him and had invited him to stay at Woodpeckers), did not hold out false hope. A year earlier she had written to him: "I am getting along all right, but would never be surprised to find myself back at Westminster [Hospital]."[31]

By spring 1953, she found she could write no longer than an hour without becoming exhausted, and at that she was dissatisfied with what she produced. Thus nothing was getting done to her satisfaction. Her overall condition was exacerbated by a constant discharge of blood. The similarity to the condition of the woman with a flow of blood in the gospel was apparent to her, but when she told Maisie why she hadn't gone earlier to the doctor, she said: "I hadn't got the humility. I was too embarrassed to tell him the symptoms."[32] One of her friends persuaded her to see the doctor, and the problem was fixed with surgery to remove uterine polyps in July. This time, she asked friends not to visit her because of the nervous strain it caused when more than one came at a time. She recuperated at the cottage, where Iris's flower garden had flourished so splendidly that she was able to make a potpourri at the end of the summer.

By December, Caryll and Iris both felt well enough to travel, and they went to Chartres for Christmas, a trip that Caryll particularly wanted to make. They had visited Chartres once before, and the experience of the cathedral remained in her mind. The weather outside was cold, and inside the cathedral it was frigid. Caryll developed a sore throat while still at Chartres, and it worsened when she returned home. Iris nursed her, and then in the usual fashion, she came down with pleurisy. Caryll, feeling slightly better, tended to her.

By early February 1954, Caryll was insisting she was no longer ill. She continued going to daily Mass at St. Mary's Cadogan Street. When she had a checkup at Westminster Hospital in the spring, the doctor told her to come back in six months. She still spent her days writing as much as she could. A periodical called *Integrity* came to her attention, and she turned her energy to writing for it. The editor's name was Dorothy Dohen, and Caryll began corresponding with her. People were still seeking her help in dealing with their neuroses and ailments. Writing to Louise Wijnhausen, the business manager of Sheed & Ward's New York office, she explained why some promised work had not yet materialized: "I am simply hunted by neurotics of all kinds who insist on coming here and talking for hours about their troubles and ailments, etc. *Guilt* has brought a positive hornet's nest (whatever that is!) on my head."[33]

In late winter of 1954, Maisie asked Caryll if she knew of any meditations on the Stations of the Cross that Sheed & Ward could publish. As it happened, the American version of the *Messenger of the Sacred Heart* had been commissioning articles from Caryll, and among them was a series on the Stations, complete with Caryll's woodcuts for each Station. The publisher immediately set about retrieving these for a book. In the meantime, Caryll had already been working on an autobiographical essay that Frank wanted for an anthology in which each chapter would be written by a person who was either born Catholic or who had entered the Church as a young child. The idea was that "they should try to convey what the experience of living in the Church has been—what has been most valuable in it, and also, if they wish, where the shoe pinches."[34]

Caryll sent the essay to Frank in the spring. When Frank read it, he told her he would like her to expand it so that it would become a book-length autobiography. Could she write another essay for the anthology? She tried to oblige over the next few weeks, and eventually sent the second attempt to Frank, who, with Maisie, was on a lecture tour throughout the United States. He replied from

California, accepting one of her pieces for the anthology (which would be published later in the year under the title *Born Catholics*; Caryll's entry was called simply "Caryll Houselander"). Frank then repeated his request for her to make some additions to the other piece so that it could become a book.

By now it was summer, and the June 1954 issue of the American journal *Integrity* was published with the theme of "Mercy." The title of Caryll's piece was "Christ's Merciful Indwelling." "I myself have had at least one rehearsal for death," she wrote, adding: "I learned from experience how the mercy of God robs death of its fear."[35]

Soon Caryll was back at Woodpeckers, carving and continuing to work on the autobiography for Frank. Iris had recently enhanced Caryll's experience of the countryside by acquiring a dog—a mongrel, part terrier, part foxhound—which they named Gregory. Sometimes Caryll kept up her amusing banter with friends who came to visit. At other times, her energy flagged. She and Iris continued to go to daily Mass, but when it rained, requiring trudging through the mud of the field, her strength failed her. She slept badly at night, and sometimes during the day she could be found in a heavy, coma-like sleep at her workbench in Woodpeckers. At times her mind seemed to be affected: she would speak very slowly, making no sense, and would drop anything that was handed to her. Willmott later told Iris that he gave her packets of Benzedrine; Caryll had given up smoking some years earlier, but she had never given up gin, and friends later wondered if she was taking the stimulant together with the liquor to keep herself going.

By August, the autobiography had a name, *A Rocking-Horse Catholic*, but was not yet finished, and although Caryll kept up some of the fiction to Frank and Maisie that her health was improving—she had been feeling so ill she was ready to die, only to be told by the doctor that she no longer had cancer—to others she admitted she was too weak to concentrate on anything. She worried that whatever work she finished now would still be unsatisfactory in Frank's eyes. Frank hired an outside reader to read what Caryll had already written. The autobiographical manuscript ended with Caryll in her late teens or early twenties, and the reader suggested that she continue where she left off, moving into the adult years. Caryll had already decided that she would not tackle this part of her life: "I honestly think it would be artistically wrong to do so, unless indeed I tried to write a real autobiography and as you know it would be impossible during the lifetime of my father and my sister."[36] Besides, she added, she had done nothing of importance and would be forgotten soon after her death.

By the middle of September the manuscript—as complete as Caryll was going to make it—had gone to the typist and was then on its way to the United States to be published. Her plan was to return to the short stories she had been working on, but the likelihood is that after the fluster and energy expended on the writing of her own early life, her stamina was depleted. She and Iris returned to London. Her fifty-third birthday came and went, and no record remains as to whether she was able to celebrate with a glass of sherry or gin and a myriad of presents and candles as she had loved to do in former years. She insisted on accompanying Iris to walk the dog and watch him chase after a ball, but she walked stiffly, as if in pain. Soon she lost all energy and remained in her flat, looked after by Iris, with the help of other friends. She was visited by Ruth and Ruth's daughter, her godchild, Deirdre. Close friends kept vigil. Gregory lay quietly by the bed. Frank and Maisie had returned from their travels, and Maisie sent for a priest to bring Communion and the oils for the last rites. Life gradually drained from her, and Caryll died on October 12, 1954.

Her funeral took place at St. Mary's Cadogan Street six days later. The night before the funeral, Caryll's coffin, draped with a black velvet pall, was brought into the church. Six candles flanked the coffin, three on either side. Burial took place in a spot chosen by Iris, overlooking a sweeping vista of rolling hills, within the burial grounds of the Anglican Church of St. Peter and St. Paul, Aylesbury. As the burial rite was taking place at the graveside, the small group accompanying the coffin noticed that a local farmer and village shopkeeper stood at a respectful distance. In a nearby field, a donkey was grazing.

Five months earlier, in Caryll's last piece of writing to be published while she was still alive, the article in *Integrity* concluded thus: "[I]n the hour of death we shall love God not with our own hearts and minds, but with the heart and the mind and the will of Christ, and with His heart and mind and will we shall long to be with God." She then ended by coming full circle to her own spiritual beginning, her final words those of Julian of Norwich:

And mercy is a work that cometh of the goodness of God. And it shall last working as long as sin is suffered to pursue rightful souls: and when sin hath no longer leave to pursue, then shall the working of mercy cease: and then shall all be brought into rightfulness, and therein stand without end.

Epilogue

Iris chose Caryll's gravestone, as well as the wording of the inscription, and had it erected not long after Caryll's death. The marker reads:

> In loving memory of
> Frances Caryll
> Houselander
> who died peacefully
> on Oct. the 12th 1954
> Grant to the soul of thy servant
> a place of cool repose
> the blessedness of quiet
> the brightness of light[1]

A short *In Memoriam* piece was written for the October 23 issue of *The Tablet* by Monsignor Ronald Knox, in which Caryll's surname was spelled incorrectly ("Houslander"). "In all she wrote, there was a candour as of childhood; she seemed to see everything for the first time, and the driest of doctrinal considerations shone out like a restored picture when she had finished with it," he wrote. "And her writing was always natural; she seemed to have no difficulty in getting the right word; no, not merely the right word, the telling word, that left you gasping. . . . There was nothing pretentious about her work, there was no self in it; you felt she imagined that anybody else could write like that if they tried. Yet every page was invigorating."[2]

On the page opposite the memorial for Caryll, an advertisement appeared for St. Thomas More School in Frensham, into which she had poured her limited energy after the war. The ad declared that the school "has achieved highly successful results" and that "it is one of the few Catholic schools in this country devoted to the education of boys whose earlier training has been retarded and who find difficulty in adapting themselves to the more conventional type of school."[3]

Caryll had appointed Frank Sheed her literary agent and gave him the authority to publish any of her yet-unpublished writings and reissue any of her books already published. A few weeks after Caryll's death, *The Stations of the Cross* was published by Sheed & Ward, with Caryll's woodcuts as the stark black-and-white Stations. In a by now familiar fashion, Caryll put the actions of each station into stark language, re-creating the action as it might actually have happened, and then enlarged her description of each station into the contemporary world, in which her readers and all who suffer now are participating in that same Passion.

The same year, Frank Sheed's *Born Catholics* was published, containing among the eighteen chapters Caryll's autobiographical essay. The next year, 1955, *A Rocking-Horse Catholic* was published in the United States. Caryll had asked Frank Sheed that the book not be published in Britain until after her father's death. American reviews were respectful, especially given the author's recent death and reviewers' memory of Caryll's clear and sharp writing. In addition, there was now a new appreciation of her background as the unhappy child of a marriage breakdown.

On October 7, 1956, Caryll's brother-in-law, Dermot Morrah, wrote to Frank with the request that Sheed & Ward reconsider publishing the book in Britain at all, for the reason that Caryll's memory was faulty: "[S]he lived, as she had done from childhood, in a world of fantasy, and was one of those people who, without intention to deceive, mistake their purely imaginative day-dreams, after which a short space of time, for events that have objectively happened."[4] Sheed & Ward, however, published the book in Britain as planned, after Willmott Houselander's death, which occurred in London on June 12, 1959.

The Jesuit scholar C. C. Martindale wrote in the British Jesuit publication *The Month* that *A Rocking-Horse Catholic*, like her other books, was "a uniquely strange and precious gift."[5] But readers of *The Tablet*, who five years earlier had read Ronald Knox's high appreciation of Caryll's works, now read, under the headline "Baffled Faith," a blistering review of *A Rocking-Horse Catholic*, written by Dominican priest Illtud Evans. It began: "The trouble about rocking-horses is that they can over-turn; at best they can scarcely be called a reliable means of getting anywhere." The reviewer went on to criticize the book's text as "a wayward commentary on a difficult childhood," seen through "the manifestly disturbed vision of a child who was both physically ill and psychologically abnormal." He went on to declare that the author "will be principally remembered for the 'rhythms' in which, with a sort of Walt Whitman prosiness, she meditated on her chosen themes." He conceded that her descriptions of the three extraordinary experiences of her youth "were plainly important for her, and they are indeed most movingly recalled," but that there was "a disturbingly hysterical note" in them. "She writes with charm of an objective experience, whether it be a visit to a theatre or the quiet days in a small convent," he wrote. "It is the religious implications that disturb her story, upset its rhythms and make one sad at the chasm that opens." The review concluded: "Publishers must be assumed to know their business, and Miss Houselander earned many readers for her verses. It does little service to her memory that what was implied needs now to be stated."[6]

It was inevitable that such a review would elicit responses. Frank Sheed replied in a letter to the editor:

Sir—In his review of Caryll Houselander's *Rocking-Horse Catholic*, Father Illtud Evans says: "Publishers must be presumed to know their own business." As he adds that the book's publication does little service to the author's memory, apparently because it makes plain how neurotic she was, we may be allowed a word of comment.

Obviously there can be any number of views of the value of Caryll Houselander's work. But we are not alone in rating it very high. Professor Mackail first discovered her and hailed her as a genius. Monsignor Knox wrote her what he called the only fan letter of his life, expressing the wish that she might conduct a school for spiritual writers.

Rocking-Horse Catholic was written before her last illness. It seems to us valuable precisely because it describes the troubled childhood and youth from which she emerged to become the remarkably well-balanced woman we knew. That great psychiatrist, Dr. Strauss, told us that he sent patients to her for social therapy, "that she might love them back to life."[7]

Two weeks later, *The Tablet* published a letter from Caryll's brother-in-law, Dermot Morrah:

Sir—I think Mr. Sheed misunderstands the reason why Father Illtud Evans, agreeing with many of us who knew my sister-in-law, Caryll Houselander, regrets his decision to publish her autobiography. It is not at all because it "makes plain how neurotic she was"; and Mr. Sheed is entitled to his belief that she became a remarkably well-balanced woman. Nor can I question the book's representation of her inward spiritual life, to which naturally she is the only competent witness.

But when Mr. Sheed finds the book "valuable precisely because it describes the troubled childhood and youth from which she emerged," I am bound to say that what is described is the childhood and youth that Caryll, living in what seemed to her friends a world of fantasy, imagined for herself much later in life. The external events she depicts had no objective reality.

It may be said, of course, that I am only pitting my memory against hers: but I shall be surprised if any of her relations or the intimate friends of her youth contradict me. I have spoken to several of these before writing this letter.[8]

Dermot Morrah, who was a member of the editorial staff at *The Times*, and had been a speech-writer for King George VI, had given Frank Sheed little to argue with, since it was not clear from his letter which events of Caryll's life she fantasized. In the meantime, Maisie Ward, whose memory of Caryll remained undimmed, decided to write a biography of her friend, and was already in the process of seeking out people close to Caryll, most of whom were still alive. Frank's brief and final letter to *The Tablet* appeared on July 2, 1960:

> Sir—I was in America when you published Mr. Morrah's comments on my letter about *A Rocking-Horse Catholic*.
> Obviously your columns are not the place for an argument between Caryll Houselander's brother-in-law and her publisher as to her mental balance. But we have been in contact with people who had known her over most of the period she covers in the book; our reasons for accepting her account of her childhood and youth will appear in the biography my wife is writing. Needless to say, any information from anyone will be welcomed.[9]

As if to shore up support for Caryll's memory, two of her friends also wrote letters to *The Tablet*. Lois Boardman, who became a friend later in Caryll's life, took issue with the reviewer's contention that Caryll would be remembered chiefly for her verses, by pointing out the titles of her books. "Many who have been helped by the compassion and humour in her long book, *Guilt*, will be glad to read this small autobiography . . . and to learn that her sympathy came from a deep understanding and personal experience," she wrote.[10] Christine Spender wrote that "our minds are selective, more especially so in the case of an artist," and gave a glimpse into

Caryll at work: "I do not forget those ever-active hands, remarkably strong-looking on such a fragile person. As she talked she carved or drew and her productions were by no means fantastic. They were as real and solid as they were artistic."[11]

In the meantime, *The Risen Christ*, a book of meditations on the Resurrection, was published in 1958. It is not clear when these meditations were written, but each displays the ease with which Caryll moves from a startling gospel insight—for example, regarding Peter's encounter with the risen Christ: "Who but Christ would have known that the one thing that could lift up that broken heart was not a formal act of contrition, but a spontaneous, almost an exasperated cry of love . . ."[12]—into a reference to everyday life. Dorothy Dohen, editor of *Integrity*, one of the last people to visit Caryll at the cottage during the summer of 1954, wrote in her review in *The Critic*: "Whether she discussed neurotics, or criminals, or war victims, or displaced and broken-hearted children, the reality of Christ's love for them in that He chose to dwell in them and identify Himself with them, was always what mattered most to her. It was her answer to darkness, desolation, misery and woe."[13]

During the late 1950s, Maisie Ward was placing notices in Catholic papers inviting correspondence from anyone who had known Caryll personally, especially during her childhood and young adulthood: the years when Maisie herself had not known Caryll. One of the periodicals that printed her request for correspondence was *The Clergy Review*, and one of the letters that came to her as a result of her request was from Mother Aloysia, the nun at St. Leonards who had become, in a sense, Caryll's savior at a crucial point in her adolescent life. Her letter indicates a lack of realization of her own pivotal role—or a humble disregard of it—in Caryll's life:

Dear Mrs. Sheed,
   Seeing your request in the October no. of the "Clergy Review," it was suggested to me by one of our nuns to write

a few words about Caryll Houselander whose prefect I was (i.e. head-mistress) while she was here at school.

At school, she was not a "mixer," but went her own way—alone seemingly, but I think far from alone as she lived her own life with God. Her school companions on the whole did not understand her. The only child with whom she appeared to be friends surprised me very much in her answer to a request the other day that she would tell me what she could remember. This lady answered me that she was not her friend, but seeing Caryll lonely, befriended her and went about with her. She found her introspective and apt to "grouse" about things in her school life.

Introspective she certainly was, but she had so much to "introspect"! When she left school—after having comforted me by telling me that I had "introduced her to Our Lord"—she wrote reams to me about her soul. I am sorry now that I did not keep her letters, but I could not foresee how really holy she was to grow and what an amazing amount of good she was to do for others.

She took early to writing holy poems for the "Messenger" and otherwise. The early ones she would send me for criticism. She copied Francis Thompson, who was at this time writing poems, holy & otherwise, with the most amazing and incomprehensible words. So I did sound her up about this, and put it to her that she would do much more good to souls by stating her deeply spiritual ideas in language that we could all understand. She took the hint sweetly as she took everything from me, and the poems gained in simplicity and were beautiful.

There is no necessity to say anything about her strenuous work in church decoration—lying on her back, on scaffolding, to paint a ceiling and such-like, and at the end of a day like this, teaching anyone, male or female, young or old, in her art studio, and never accepting a penny from them, her one idea being, in this way, able to get into contact with them and help their souls. All this from someone with poor health at the best of times—you must know all this, and all about her books.

She had a delightful dry sense of humour. I was shopping with her once in the crowded Regent St. area, and I found that when crossing the road, I always got over to the other side before her, leaving her still awaiting her opportunity on the other side. This having happened several times, I at length asked her why she didn't take her chance sooner like I did. In her dry serious kind of drawl she answered: "Well, of course, Mother, if you *like* to take your life into your own hands, I can't help it!" (Being a country cousin, and she a Londoner, it just *might* have been necessary for my angel guardian to work strenuously to keep me safe!) I couldn't help laughing, but she wasn't at all convinced by my logical argument that I had come safely across each time.

Then came her cancer, and she wrote from the hospital with the calm statement: "I have cancer; well, if God wants me to die it's all right." You will know all the details as to her death. I think she got better and came home, but eventually died of her disease in hospital, and I feel sure, went straight to heaven. I shall much look forward to a biography. . . .

Please excuse scratchings-out and hasty scribble. I cannot type and I don't think this is worth bothering anyone else to type it. I was very fond of the child, and she has said many a thing to me that has rung a bell in my heart.

Yours very sincerely in J.C.,
Mother Aloysia S.H.C.J.[14]

Maisie Ward's biography of Caryll, *Caryll Houselander: That Divine Eccentric*, was published by Sheed & Ward in 1962, the subtitle taken from Dr. Strauss's description of Caryll in a letter he had written to Maisie. Then, *The Letters of Caryll Houselander: Her Spiritual Legacy*, edited by Maisie Ward, was published in

1965. This was a sampling of Caryll's correspondence, in which she displays the best of her compassionate self. The letters reveal a friend who is at once challenging, insightful, and gentle, displaying the gift of clarity which makes her best writing so readable and profound. The same year, 1965, saw the closing of the Second Vatican Council and the publication of the Council's decrees after three years of deliberation. What is left unwritten is Caryll's thinking in response to the Council and the sweeping changes in the Catholic Church: what she might have thought, what she might have written.

Caryll's grave, Church of St. Peter and St. Paul, Ellesborough, Bucks. Photo by Mary Francis Coady.

Acknowledgments

My primary thanks are to Bernard Kingvisser and Sarah King Head, Executors of the Estate of Margot King, and Emily Kingvisser, for generously trusting me with full access to the late medieval scholar Margot King's research materials on the life and work of Caryll Houselander. My deep gratitude to them.

Thanks as well to Virginia and Catherine Utley, grand-nieces of Caryll Houselander, for their gracious support of this biography, and to the Utley family for permission to publish early photographs of her; to Professor Marie Ann Mayeski for sending me helpful material and answering my Caryll Houselander-related questions; to Father Ronald Cafeo of the Madonna House Apostolate for sending me documents relating to the life and work of Yvonne Bosch van Drakestein; to Marian Ronan for background help related to the history of the Grail movement; to Father Keith Sawyer for taking me to Caryll Houselander's grave; to Sister Judith Lancaster SHCJ and Isabel Keating for permission to publish the letter of Mother Aloysia SHCJ to Maisie Ward; to Camilla Shivarg, granddaughter of Iris Wyndham, for permission to publish photographs from her grandmother's collection.

The following archivists were helpful to me, and I am grateful for their patient replies to emailed questions: Joe Smith, University of Notre Dame Archives; Isabel Keating, Archivist for the Society of the Holy Child Jesus, European Province; Mary Allen, Jesuits in Britain Archives; Noel S. McFarran, Caryll Houselander Collection, Special Collections, John M. Kelly Library, University of St. Michael's College.

A month spent at Studium in the College of St. Benedict, St. Joseph, Minnesota, allowed me to work on the final parts of this biography. I am grateful to Sister Ann Biermaier, director of Studium, as well as the entire community at St. Benedict's Monastery.

A travel grant from the Cushwa Center for the Study of American Catholicism enabled me to consult the Caryll Houselander documents and the Sheed & Ward papers at the University of Notre Dame Archives. My gratitude to the Cushwa Center for this grant.

Finally, many thanks to Robert Ellsberg, Jon Sweeney, Maria Angelini, and all at Orbis Books.

Notes

1. A ROCKING-HORSE BEGINNING (1901–1917)

[1]Christine Spender to Maisie Ward (hereafter cited as MW), Sheed & Ward Family Papers (hereafter cited as CSWD) 12/13, University of Notre Dame Archives (hereafter cited as UNDA).

[2]Caryll Houselander (hereafter cited as CH) to MW, August 29, 1954, Caryll Houselander Archives (hereafter cited as CHLD), UNDA.

[3]Rosamond Batchelor to MW, May 19, 1961, CSWD, 12/13, UNDA.

[4]Caryll Houselander, *A Rocking-Horse Catholic* (New York: Sheed & Ward, 1943), 4.

[5]Ibid., 3.

[6]Ruth Morrah, Letter to the Editor, *The Tablet* 216, no. 6391 (November 17, 1962): 12–13.

[7]Ruth Morrah to MW, January 22, 1961, CSWD 12/13, UNDA.

[8]*A Rocking-Horse Catholic,* 9.

[9]Ibid.

[10]Ibid., 15.

[11]Ruth Morrah to MW, January 22, 1961, CSWD 12/13, UNDA.

[12]CH to Smoky, quoted in *Caryll and Smoky* (unfinished manuscript by Maisie Ward), CSWD 15/04, UNDA.

[13]*A Rocking-Horse Catholic,* 31.

[14]Ibid., 32.

[15]Letter from a one-time friend, Marguerita Feddon, to Maisie Ward, September 25, 1958: "I heard she [Gertrude Houselander] lived in Clifton in the Pro-Cathedral parish but usually went to St. Mary's-on-the-Quay—very friendly with Father Carolan SJ." CSWD 12/13, UNDA.

[16]The psychiatrist Jerome Kroll ("Caryll Houselander's Childhood Neurosis," *Vox Benedictina* 2, no. 1 [1985]: 74–80) suggests that the origin of Caryll's illness may have been rheumatic fever.

[17]Ruth Morrah to MW, January 22, 1961, CSWD 12/13, UNDA.

[18]Caryll Houselander, "Ghosts and Memories," unpublished manuscript, CHLD 1/06, UNDA.

[19]*The Oltonian: Our Lady of Compassion School Magazine,* no. 2, February 1913.

[20]Maisie Ward, *Caryll Houselander: That Divine Eccentric* (London: Sheed & Ward, 1962). Maisie Ward, who visited the school in the late 1950s, wrote that the nuns remembered Sister Mary Benedicta as cultured and well educated (45).

[21]F. J. Sheed, ed., *Born Catholics* (London: Sheed & Ward, 1954), 254.

[22]*A Rocking-Horse Catholic,* 74.

[23]Morrah, Letter to the Editor, *The Tablet,* 216, no. 6391 (November 17, 1962): 12–13.

[24]*Born Catholics,* 256.

[25]CH to Smoky, in *Caryll and Smoky,* CSWD 15/04, UNDA.

[26]*A Rocking-Horse Catholic,* 94.

[27]Ibid., 95–96.

[28]Archives of Society of the Holy Child Jesus, European Province.

[29]Mother Aloysia to MW, November 12, 1958, CSWD 12/13, UNDA.

2. SUMMONED TO LONDON (1918–1922)

[1]Martin Gilbert, *The First World War: A Complete History* (New York: Henry Holt, 1994), 403.

[2]CH to Smoky, March 29, 1918, quoted in *Caryll and Smoky* (unfinished manuscript by Maisie Ward), CSWD 15/04, UNDA.

[3]*A Rocking-Horse Catholic,* 112.

[4]*Born Catholics,* 260.

[5]CH to Smoky, 22 July 1918, quoted in *Caryll and Smoky,* CSWD 15/04, UNDA.

[6]CH to Smoky, undated, quoted in *Caryll and Smoky,* CSWD 15/04, UNDA.

[7]CH to Smoky, June 1919, quoted in *Caryll and Smoky,* CSWD 15/04, UNDA.

[8]Quoted in *Rebecca West: A Life,* by Victoria Glendinning (London: Weidenfeld and Nicolson, 1987), 131.

[9]Valentine Ackland to MW, CSWD 15/04, UNDA.

[10]Dermot Morrah to Frank Sheed, 7 October 1956. CSWD 12/14, UNDA.

[11]Robin Bruce Lockhart, *Reilly: Ace of Spies* (London: Penguin, 1967), 112.

[12]Ibid., 113.

[13]Edward van der Rhoer, *Master Spy: A True Story of Allied Espionage in Bolshevik Russia* (New York: Charles Scribner's Sons, 1981), 146.

[14]"Spiritual Journal," CSWD 12/11, UNDA.

[15]*Messenger of the Sacred Heart,* 20 February 1930, 59.

[16]*The Letters of Caryll Houselander,* ed. Maisie Ward (New York: Sheed & Ward, 1965), 108–9.

[17]Quoted in a letter from Robin Bruce Lockhart to Margot King, August 28, 1995. The Estate of Margot King.

[18]The British television mini-series *Reilly: Ace of Spies,* based on Lockhart's first book, was produced in 1983 with the actor Sam Neill as Sidney Reilly. The actress Joanne Pearce appears in brief scenes as Caryll Houselander.

[19]*A Rocking-Horse Catholic,* 131.

[20]Ibid., 140.

3. SEARCH FOR GOD (1923–1929)

[1]Dana Greene, *The Living of Maisie Ward* (Notre Dame, IN: University of Notre Dame Press, 1997), 69.

[2]*St. Leonards Chronicle,* 1924, Archives of the Society of the Holy Child Jesus, European Province.

[3]*The Times,* November 28, 1924, 5.

[4]Iris told Maisie Ward that she invited Caryll to live at Bacombe Warren (*Caryll Houselander: That Divine Eccentric,* 79). In *Dawn Chorus* (London: Virago, 2004), Joan Wyndham does not include Caryll among those living at Bacombe Warren. She writes that Caryll invited herself to live at Evelyn Gardens (68–70).

[5]Caryll is sometimes referred to as a lesbian, as in the obituary of Joan Wyndham (*The Guardian,* April 16, 2007). Jean E. Kennard, author of *Vera Brittain and Winifred Holtby: A Working Partnership* (Hanover: University Press of New Hampshire, 1989), explains that confusion can arise when the word "lesbian" is used, because no one exact definition is used. In the late nineteenth and early twentieth centuries—and perhaps especially immediately after World War I—women "frequently formed lasting, primary emotional bonds with other women that were often expressed in passionate language though probably not in sexual contact" (7–8).

[6]CH to Yvonne Bosch van Drakestein, August 26, 1939, CHLD 2/01, UNDA.

[7]As an author, Father Steuart was known as RHJ Steuart.

[8]John Saward, John Morrill, and Michael Tomko, eds., *Firmly I Believe and Truly: The Spiritual Tradition of Catholic England* (New York: Oxford University Press, 2013), 572.

[9]Katharine Kendall, *The Spiritual Teaching of Father Steuart* (London: Burns & Oates, 1952), 92.

[10]CSWD 12/11, UNDA.

[11] *Our Dead,* British Jesuit Archives & Collections, 336.

[12] CHLD 1/08, UNDA.

[13] CHLD 1/09, UNDA.

[14] Nothing more is known about this relationship.

[15] Rosamond Batchelor to MW, CSWD 12/13, UNDA.

[16] CH to MW, September 3, 1944, CSWD 12/12, UNDA.

[17] CSWD 12/11, UNDA.

4. CALM LEADING TO STORM THREAT (1930–1939)

[1] According to Wilfred Sheed, Caryll never showed her teeth "because she thought teeth looked silly" (*Frank and Maisie: A Memoir with Parents* [New York: Simon and Schuster, 1985, 196).

[2] CH to Christine Spender, March 2, 1946, *The Letters of Caryll Houselander,* 103.

[3] Eventually, according to Wilfred Sheed, his father, Frank, would use Caryll's handwriting analysis "on a couple of handwriting specimens, and . . . she had flushed out deeply buried secrets which later checked out" (*Frank and Maisie,* 196).

[4] Joan Wyndham's memories of Caryll ("Baby" or "Sid", as she knew her) can be found in her four books of diaries and memoir: *Love Lessons* (1985), *Love Is Blue* (1986), *Anything Once* (1992), and *Dawn Chorus* (2004).

[5] "Yvonne Bosch van Drakestein" (obituary), by Derek Worlock, Archbishop of Liverpool, *The Tablet* 248, no. 8036 (August 13, 1994): 1031.

[6] Yvonne Bosch van Drakestein, interview with Father Ron Cafeo, Madonna House, Combermere, Ontario, Canada, July 1978.

[7] CH to Mrs. Boardman, November 19, 1946, *The Letters of Caryll Houselander,* 144.

[8] "Mother Julian of Norwich," *New Blackfriars* 15, no.168 (March 1934): 177.

[9] CH to Yvonne Bosch von Drakestein, 2 September 1939, CHLD 2/01, UNDA.

[10] "Mother Julian of Norwich," 184.

[11] R. H. J. Steuart, SJ, *Diversity in Holiness* (London: Sheed & Ward, 1938), 14.

[12] CH to Mr. St. George, *The Letters of Caryll Houselander,* 4.

[13] CH to Elizabeth Billaux, 30 September 1935, CHLD 2/01, UNDA.

[14] *St. Leonards Chronicler* (1930): 24, Archives of the Society of the Holy Child Jesus, European Province.

[15] *The Pylon* 3, no. 3 (July 1936): 19–20, Archives of the Society of the Holy Child Jesus, European Province.

[16] *The Letters of Caryll Houselander,* 65.

[17] Among Caryll's books was a well-marked biography, *Bramwell Booth,* by Catherine Bramwell Booth (London: Rich & Cowan, 1933).

[18] Rosamond Batchelor to MW, CSWD 12/13, UNDA.

[19] Ibid.

[20] Wyndham, *Dawn Chorus,* 150.

[21] Ibid., 195.

[22] CSWD 12/11, UNDA.

[23] Cf. "The Mystical Body": "The doctrine of the Mystical Incorporation of the Christian with Christ may well be considered as the foundation and summing up of the entire Christian system both in theory and in practice" (*The Two Voices: Spiritual Conferences of R. H. J. Steuart, SJ*, edited with a memoir by C. C. Martindale, SJ [Westminster, MD: Newman Press, 1952], 197).

[24] *The Grail,* January/February 1955, acknowledged to have been written by Caryll in the late 1930s.

[25] Wyndham, *Dawn Chorus,* 231.

[26] Ibid., 232.

[27] CH to Yvonne Bosch van Drakestein, August 26, 1939, CHLD 2/01, UNDA.

[28] Ibid., *The Letters of Caryll Houselander,* 23.

[29] Ibid., August 31, 1939.

[30] CH to Yvonne Bosch van Drakestein, September 1, 1939, CHLD 2/01, UNDA.

[31] Ibid., September 3, 1939.

[32] Ibid., September 6, 1939.

[33] Ibid., September 12, 1939.

[34] Ibid., September 17, 1939.

[35] Ibid., September 21, 1939.

[36] Ibid., October 1, 1939.

[37] Ibid., September 21, 1939.

5. WAR (1940–1945)

[1] Mollie Panter-Downes, *London War Notes, 1939–1945* (New York: Farrar, Straus & Giroux, 1971), 98.

[2] CH quoted in Maisie Ward, *Unfinished Business* (London: Sheed & Ward, 1964), 220–21.

[3] *New Six O'Clock Saints* (New York: Sheed & Ward, 1945).

[4] CH to Henry Tayler, December 27, 1940, CHLD 2/01, UNDA.

[5] W. Sheed, *Frank and Maisie,* 61.

[6] Ibid., 57.

[7]CH to Henry Tayler, December 12, 1940, CHLD 2/01, UNDA.

[8]Ibid., January 13, 1942, CHLD 2/01, UNDA.

[9]CH to Henry Tayler, December 27, 1940, *The Letters of Caryll Houselander,* 71.

[10]The conflagration known as the Great Fire of London took place as flames originating in a bakery swept through the center of the city over a four-day period in September 1666.

[11]Wyndham, *Love Lessons,* 166.

[12]Maisie Ward, *This Burning Heat* (New York: Sheed & Ward, 1941), 106–7.

[13]Ibid., 102–3.

[14]Ibid., 106.

[15]Caryll Houselander, *This War Is the Passion* (London: Sheed & Ward, 1943), 1.

[16]An announcement in *The Grail* indicated that as a result of *This War Is the Passion,* "the Grail spirit is being brought to thousands of Americans who otherwise would not have come in contact with it" (*The Grail* 9, no. 2 [1942]: 13).

[17]*Canadian Register,* April 11, 1942, 7.

[18]*This War Is the Passion,* 75.

[19]CH to Henry Tayler, November 2, 1942, CHLD 2/01, UNDA.

[20]CH to Henry Tayler, April 27, 1942, *The Letters of Caryll Houselander,* 79.

[21]Ibid., January 14, 1941, CHLD 2/01, UNDA.

[22]Ibid., January 13, 1942, CHLD 2/01, UNDA.

[23]Ibid., July 20, 1949, CHLD 2/01, UNDA.

[24]Ibid., January 13, 1942, CHLD 2/01, UNDA.

[25]Ibid., December 6, 1941, CHLD, 2/01, UNDA.

[26]Christine Spender to MW, CSWD 12/13, UNDA.

[27]CH to Archie Campbell-Murdoch, November 26, 1941, *The Letters of Caryll Houselander,* 39.

[28]CH to Elizabeth Billaux, October 20, 1942, CHLD 2/01, UNDA.

[29]CH quoted in Ward, *Caryll Houselander: That Divine Eccentric,* 168.

[30]Winston Churchill: "This is not the end. It is not even the beginning of the end. But it is, perhaps, the end of the beginning." November 10, 1942.

[31]CH to Archie Campbell-Murdoch, May 10, 1942, CHLD 2/01, UNDA.

[32]Frank Sheed to MW, July 27, 1943, CSWD 1/07, UNDA.

[33]CH to Henry Tayler, April 30, 1942, CHLD 2/01, UNDA.

[34]CH to Henry Tayler, December 28, 1942, CHLD 2/01, UNDA.

[35]CH to Archie Campbell-Murdoch, January 29, 1943, CHLD 2/01, UNDA.

[36]CH to Henry Tayler, January 8, 1944, CHLD 2/01, UNDA.

[37]Ibid., June 23, 1944, CHLD 2/01, UNDA.

[38]CH to Frank Sheed, April 29, 1944, 12/12, UNDA.

[39]Caryll Houselander, *The Reed of God* (London: Sheed & Ward, 1976), xi.

[40]Ibid., 5.

[41]Ibid., 27.

[42]Ibid., 42.

[43]In the 2006 edition of *The Reed of God* (Ave Maria Press), the foreword by Marie Anne Mayeski refers to four guidelines for Marian devotion issued by Pope Paul VI as elucidated by the theologian Elizabeth A. Johnson in her book, *Truly Our Sister:* A genuine and sound Mariology should have a solid biblical character; be marked by a liturgical sensitivity rooted in Eucharistic worship, attentive to the liturgical seasons; be ecumenical, its focus on the mysteries of Christ; and be attentive to the contemporary conditions in which people, especially women, live. *The Reed of God*, Mayeski says, ticks all boxes. It also anticipates some of the theological principles flowing from Vatican II for a renewed theology of Mary.

[44]Frank Sheed to MW, October 10, 1944, CSWD 1/07, UNDA.

[45]CH to MW, April 21, 1944, CSWD 12/12, UNDA.

[46]Ibid., May 24, 1944, CSWD 12/12, UNDA.

[47]Ibid., September 12, 1944, CSWD 12/12, UNDA.

[48]Ibid.

[49]Frank Sheed to MW, April 19, 1944, CSWD 1/07, UNDA.

[50]CH to Archie Campbell-Murdoch, October 17, 1944, CHLD 2/01, UNDA.

[51]Greene, *The Living of Maisie Ward*, 107.

[52]CH to MW, September 3, 1944, CSWD 12/12, UNDA.

[53]CH to MW, September 20, 1944, CSWD 12/12, UNDA.

[54]CH to MW, September 8, 1944, CSWD 12/12, UNDA.

6. POSTWAR (1945–1949)

[1]CH to Archie Campbell-Murdoch, January 24, 1945, UNDA.

[2]*The Reed of God*, 73.

[3]CH to Archie Campbell-Murdoch, January 24, 1945, UNDA.

[4]Panter-Downes, *London War Notes*, 376.

[5]Wyndham, *Love Is Blue*, 178.

[6]CH to MW, May 10, 1945, CSWD 12/12, UNDA.

[7]Ibid.

[8]An annual pilgrimage walk commemorating the route walked by the sixteenth- and seventeenth-century martyrs to be executed at Tyburn.

[9]Prayer for the first joyful mystery in Maisie Ward and Caryll Houselander,

The Splendour of the Rosary (New York: Sheed & Ward, 1945), 65.

[10]Caryll Houselander, *The Flowering Tree* (New York: Sheed & Ward, 1945): "From a Letter to Maisie Ward" (no page number).

[11]Ibid., "Author's Note" (no page number).

[12]Ibid., 58.

[13]CH to Henry Tayler, December 23, 1945, CHLD 2/01, UNDA.

[14]Ward, *Caryll Houselander: That Divine Eccentric,* 206.

[15]W. Sheed, *Frank and Maisie,* 196–97.

[16]CH to Henry Tayler, November 11, 1945, CHLD 2/01, UNDA.

[17]CH to MW, April 23, 1947, CSWD 12/12, UNDA.

[18]CH to "A Friend with a Nervous Illness," in *The Letters of Caryll Houselander,* 209.

[19]CH to "A Young Friend Who Married and Settled Abroad," ibid., 126.

[20]Caryll Houselander, *The Dry Wood* (Washington, DC: Catholic University of America Press, 2022), 117–18.

[21]Ibid., 140–41.

[22]Ibid., 59–60.

[23]Ibid., 179.

[24]Ibid., 69.

[25]Ibid., 46.

[26]*The Downside Review* 66 (April 1948): 228.

[27]*The Sewanee Review* 56, no. 2 (Spring 1948): 354–55.

[28]Caryll Houselander, *The Comforting of Christ* (New York: Sheed & Ward, 1947), 2.

[29]CH to Archie Campbell–Murdoch, September 14, 1947, CHLD 2/01.

[30]CH to Mrs. Boardman, February 17, 1954, *The Letters of Caryll Houselander.*

[31]CH to Henry Tayler, April 11, 1948, CHLD 2/01, UNDA.

[32]CH to MW, July 14, 1948, CSWD 12/12, UNDA.

[33]CH to Henry Tayler, February 18, 1949, CHLD 2/01, UNDA.

[34]CH to MW, March 23, 1948, CSWD 12/12, UNDA.

[35]*America* 81 (May 28, 1949): 292.

[36]Caryll Houselander, *The Passion of the Infant Christ* (New York: Sheed & Ward, 1949), 12.

[37]Ibid., 13.

[38]*Life in the Spirit* 4 (1949): 280.

[39]W. Sheed, *Frank and Maisie: A Memoir with Parents,* 197.

[40]CH to Archie Campbell-Murdoch, September 30, 1948, CHLD 2/01, UNDA.

[41]CH to Archie Campbell-Murdoch, May 13, 1949, CHLD 2/01, UNDA.

[42]CH to Henry Tayler, June 1, 1949, CHLD 2/01, UNDA.

[43]Ibid., June 14, 1949, CHLD 2/01, UNDA.

[44]CH to Archie Campbell-Murdoch, December 26, 1949, CHLD 2/01, UNDA.

7. FINAL JOURNEY (1950–1954)

[1]CH to Henry Tayler, March 9, 1950, CHLD 2/01, UNDA.

[2]Ibid., March 29, 1950.

[3]Foreword to *Reproachfully Yours,* by Lucile Hasley (New York: Sheed & Ward, 1949), x.

[4]CH to Henry Tayler, March 9, 1950, CHLD 2/01, UNDA.

[5]CH to Frank Sheed and MW, November 25, 1950, CSWD 12/12, UNDA.

[6]Rosamond Batchelor to MW, CSWD 12/13, UNDA.

[7]CH to Archie Campbell-Murdoch, March 27, 1951, CHLD 2/01, UNDA.

[8]CH to Louise Wijnhausen, February 21, 1951, CHLD 2/02, UNDA.

[9]CH to MW, April 5, 1951, CSWD 12/12, UNDA.

[10]CH to MW and Frank Sheed, April 24, 1952, CSWD 12/12, UNDA.

[11]CH to Archie Campbell-Murdoch, March 27, 1951, CHLD 2/01, UNDA.

[12]CH to MW, April 5, 1951, CSWD 12/12, UNDA.

[13]CH to Diana (Dickie) Orpen, April 5, 1951, CHLD 2/01, UNDA.

[14]Diana (Dickie) Orpen to MW, July 21, 1960, CSWD 12/13, UNDA.

[15]CH to Henry Tayler, July 21, 1948, CHLD 2/01, UNDA.

[16]Caryll Houselander, *Guilt* (1952; New York: Gordian Press, 1971), 29.

[17]Ibid., xi.

[18]Ibid., 15.

[19]Ibid., 17.

[20]Ibid., 77.

[21]Ibid., 101–2.

[22]*Integrity,* December 1951, 34.

[23]Ibid., 35.

[24]*Renascence* 4 (April 1952): 201–2.

[25]*Catholic Times,* March 7, 1952.

[26]Imprimatur page of *Guilt.*

[27]Ward, *Unfinished Business*, 351.

[28]Yvonne would eventually go on to work in the liturgical renewal of the Church, assisting the bishops of England and Wales, and helping with the translation of psalms that had been put to music by the composer Joseph Gelineau, which would become known as the "Grail Psalms." After a change

in leadership in the English Grail in the late 1960s, she retired to Madonna House in Combermere, Ontario, Canada, dying on August 2, 1994.

[29]CH to Yvonne Bosch van Drakestein, July 8, 1951, CHLD 2/01, UNDA.
[30]Diana (Dickie) Orpen to MW, July 21, 1960, CSWD 12/13, UNDA.
[31]CH to Dr. Begg, January 21, 1952, CHLD 2/01, UNDA.
[32]CH to MW, July 13, 1953, CSWD 12/12, UNDA.
[33]CH to Louise Wijnhausen, March 26, 1954, CHLD 2/01, UNDA.
[34]Sheed, *Born Catholics*, 3.
[35]*Integrity* 8&9 (June 1954): 27.
[36]CH to MW and Frank Sheed, August 29, 1954, CSWD 12/12, UNDA.

EPILOGUE

[1]Iris died in March 1974. Her grave is not far from Caryll's.
[2]"Miss Caryll Houselander," *The Tablet* 204, no. 5970 (October 23, 1954): 408.
[3]Ibid., 409.
[4]Dermot Morrah to Frank Sheed, October 7, 1956, CSWD 15/04.
[5]"The Mystery of Faith," *The Month* 25, no. 1 (January 1961): 57.
[6]"Baffled Faith," by Illtud Evans, O.P., *The Tablet* 214, no. 6258 (April 30, 1960), 420.
[7]"Rocking-Horse Catholic," *The Tablet* 214, no. 6260 (May 14, 1960): 475.
[8]"Rocking-Horse Catholic," *The Tablet* 214, no. 6262 (May 28, 1960): 523.
[9]"A Rocking-Horse Catholic," *The Tablet* 214, no. 6267 (July 2, 1960): 633.
[10]*The Tablet* 214, no. 6260 (May 14, 1960): 475.
[11]*The Tablet* 214, no. 6264 (June 4, 1960): 523.
[12]Caryll Houselander, *The Risen Christ* (London: Sheed & Ward, 1958), 43.
[13]*The Critic* 16, no. 6 (March 1958), 44.
[14]Mother Aloysia to MW, November 12, 1958, CSWD 12/13, UNDA.

References

Ackroyd, Peter. *London: The Biography.* London: Chatto & Windus, 2000.

Bassett, Bernard, SJ. *The English Jesuits from Campion to Martindale.* New York: Herder & Herder, 1967.

Brown, Alden V. *The Grail Movement and American Catholicism, 1940–1975.* Notre Dame, IN: University of Notre Dame Press, 1989.

Cook, Andrew. *Ace of Spies: The True Story of Sidney Reilly.* Stroud, UK: Tempus, 2002.

Dakers, Caroline. *Clouds: The Biography of a Country House.* New Haven, CT: Yale University Press, 1991.

Gilbert, Martin. *The First World War: A Complete History.* New York: Henry Holt, 1994.

Glendinning, Victoria. *Rebecca West: A Life.* London: Weidenfeld and Nicolson, 1987.

Greene, Dana. *The Living of Maisie Ward.* Notre Dame, IN: University of Notre Dame Press, 1997.

Greene, Dana. "Maisie Ward as 'Theologian,'" in *Women & Theology,* ed. Mary Ann Hinsdale and Phyllis Kaminski, 50–61. Maryknoll, NY: Orbis Books, 1995.

Harmon, Katharine E. *There Were Also Many Women There.* Collegeville, MN: Liturgical Press, 2012.

Hastings, Adrian. *A History of English Christianity: 1920–1985.* London, UK: Collins, 1986.

Houselander, Caryll. "Caryll Houselander," in *Born Catholics,* ed. Frank Sheed. New York: Sheed & Ward, 1954.

Houselander, Caryll. *The Comforting of Christ.* New York: Sheed & Ward, 1947.

Houselander, Caryll. *The Dry Wood.* New York: Sheed & Ward, 1947.

Houselander, Caryll. *The Flowering Tree.* New York: Sheed & Ward, 1945.

Houselander, Caryll. Foreword to *Reproachfully Yours,* by Lucile Hasley. New York: Sheed & Ward, 1949.

Houselander, Caryll. *Guilt.* 1952. New York: Gordian Press, 1971.

Houselander, Caryll. *The Letters of Caryll Houselander.* Edited by Maisie Ward. New York: Sheed & Ward, 1965.

Houselander, Caryll. *The Passion of the Infant Christ.* New York: Sheed & Ward, 1949.

Houselander, Caryll. *The Reed of God.* 8th British ed. London: Sheed & Ward, 1976.

Houselander, Caryll. *The Risen Christ.* London: Sheed & Ward, 1958.

Houselander, Caryll. *A Rocking-Horse Catholic.* New York: Sheed & Ward, 1955.

Houselander, Caryll. *This War Is the Passion.* London: Sheed & Ward, 1943.

Kalvan, Janet. *Women Breaking Boundaries: A Grail Journey, 1940–1995.* Albany: State University of New York Press, 1999.

Kendall, Katharine. *Father Steuart: A Study of His Life and Teaching.* London, UK: Burns & Oates, 1950.

Kendall, Katharine. *Spiritual Teaching of Father Steuart.* London: Burns & Oates, 1952.

Kennard, Jean E. *Fera Brittain and Winifred Holtby: A Working Partnership.* Hanover: University Press of New Hampshire, 1989.

Kroll, Dr. Jerome. "Caryll Houselander's Childhood Neurosis." *Vox Benedictina* 2, no. 1 (1985): 74–80.

Lander Johnson, Bonnie, and Julia Meszaros. Introduction to *The Dry Wood,* by Caryll Houselander. Washington, DC: Catholic University of America Press, 2022.

Lockhart, Robin Bruce. *Reilly: Ace of Spies*. London: Penguin, 1967.

O'Boyle, Patrick J. "Frank Sheed on the Stump." *Commonweal,* April 23, 1999, 16–17.

Orpen, Diana. *Meditations with a Pencil*. New York: Sheed & Ward, 1946.

Panter-Downes, Mollie. *London War Notes*. New York: Farrar, Straus & Giroux, 1971.

Renton, Claudia. *Those Wild Wyndhams*. London, UK: William Collins, 2014.

Ronan, Marian, and Mary O'Brien. *Women of Vision: Sixteen Founders of the International Grail Movement*. Berkeley, CA: Apocryphile Press, 2017.

Saward, John, John Morrill, and Michael Tomko, eds. *Firmly I Believe and Truly: The Spiritual Tradition of Catholic England*. New York: Oxford University Press, 2013.

Sheed, F. J. *The Instructed Heart*. Huntington, IN: Our Sunday Visitor, 1979.

Sheed, F. J., ed. *Born Catholics*. London, UK: Sheed & Ward, 1954.

Sheed, Wilfred. *Frank and Maisie: A Memoir with Parents*. New York: Simon and Schuster, 1985.

Spoerl, Kelley. "Caryll Houselander: Divine Eccentric and Prophet of Vatican II." *The Way* 54, no. 1 (January 2015): 51–64.

Steuart, R. H. J, SJ. *Diversity in Holiness*. London: Sheed & Ward, 1938.

Steuart, R. H. J., SJ. "Mother Julian of Norwich." *New Blackfriars* 15, no. 168 (March 1934).

Steuart, R.H.J., SJ. *The Two Voices: Spiritual Conferences of R.H.J. Steuart, S.J.,* edited with a Memoir by C. C. Martindale, S.J. Westminster, MD: Newman Press, 1952.

Van der Rhoer, Edward. *Master Spy: A True Story of Allied Espionage in Bolshevik Russia*. New York: Charles Scribner's Sons, 1981.

Ward, Maisie. *Caryll Houselander: That Divine Eccentric*. London: Sheed & Ward, 1962.

Ward, Maisie. *This Burning Heat*. New York: Sheed & Ward, 1941.

Ward, Maisie. *To and Fro on the Earth*. London: Catholic Book Club, 1973.

Ward, Maisie. *Unfinished Business.* London: Sheed & Ward, 1964.

Ward, Maisie, and Caryll Houselander. *The Splendour of the Rosary.* New York: Sheed & Ward, 1945.

Wyndham, Joan. *Anything Once.* London: Flamingo HarperCollins, 1993.

Wyndham, Joan. *Dawn Chorus.* London: Virago Press, 2004.

Wyndham, Joan. *Love Is Blue: A Wartime Diary.* Glasgow: Fontana Paperbacks, 1987.

Wyndham, Joan. *Love Lessons: A Wartime Journal.* Glasgow: Fontana Paperbacks, 1986.

Index